BELIEVERS NEED THE GOSPEL

CALVARY PRESS
PO Box 805
Amityville, NY 11701
calvarypress.com

BELIEVERS NEED THE GOSPEL

Peter Jeffery

Calvary Press Publishing
P.O. Box 805
Amityville, NY 11701
U.S.A.
1 (800) 789-8175 / calvarypress.com
ISBN 1-879737-42-6

For information address the publishers—
Calvary Press Publishing P.O. Box 805 Amityville, NY 11701

Cover & Page Design: Anthony Rotolo

Jeffery, Peter
    Believers Need the Gospel
Recommended Dewey Decimal Classification: 234
Suggested Subject Headings:
1. Christian Living—Christianity—Gospel
2. Religion—Christian Growth—Salvation
I. Title

Manufactured in the United States of America
    1 2 3 4 5 6 7 8 9 10   00 01 02 03

CONTENTS

INTRODUCTION

Christians are what they are because of the gospel. When they first heard the good news that God loved them and sent the Lord Jesus Christ to pay the ransom price for their sin, it sounded *too* good to be true. But the more they became convicted of sin, the more they longed for the gospel message to be real. When it finally dawned on their soul that it's true—the joy, relief and thrill were beyond description. God loved them, Christ died for them, and they were now saved from the guilt and consequence of sin, which is judgement and hell. Lines in hymns that previously were meaningless now took on a whole new significance:

> Jesus shall take the highest honor.
> Great is the gospel of our glorious God.
> You are beautiful beyond description.
> Amazing grace! How sweet the sound
> that saved a wretch like me!

These words summed up exactly how they felt. During the first few weeks of being a Christian they couldn't get enough of the gospel; they were captivated by its message. Gradually they began to settle into their new Christian life and began to learn the need for holiness and discipleship. The Bible's teaching on things like prayer, faithfulness, obedience, and worship occupied their thinking and longings, but imperceptibly, perhaps, there grew in them a tendency to lose the simple thrill of being saved. They became accustomed to the gospel and thought they had outgrown their need for it. That message was for sinners and they now needed more than it offered.

Sadly, this is a common experience for many Christians in our age. It's true that they need more than sermons on "You must be born again," and "For God so loved the world," but if they lose the wonder and thrill of the gospel, they have serious spiritual problems. Christians need the gospel as well as unbelievers. Whether we have been saved for two weeks or twenty years, we all need to regularly hear the message of the cross and the grace and love of God in and through the Lord Jesus Christ. We need it because everything else in the Christian life flows out of it and depends upon it for freshness and vitality. That's why there's nothing more thrilling to a believer than to hear the gospel preached in the power of the Holy Spirit. It melts the heart and stirs the soul—and may even cause him or her to want, if it were possible, to be converted all over again. If we lose sight of the cross and all that the New Testament teaches as to its meaning and significance, we will be floundering spiritually. We may still go through the motions of Christian activity, but we ourselves will be spiritually dry and barren. The gospel is crucial to a healthy Christian life—that's why Christians need the Gospel. This book is not written to teach the believer any new insight, but, rather, to remind them of Jesus and the cross, and the glorious salvation God has given us. Its ultimate aim is to promote holiness in individual Christians, and therefore strengthen the churches. This, however, will not be achieved if we forget "the rock from which you were cut and the quarry from which you were hewn" (Isaiah 51:1).

> Tell me the story slowly,
> That I may take it in—
> That wonderful redemption,
> God's remedy for sin.
> Tell me the story often,
> For I forget so soon;
> The early dew of morning
> Has passed away at noon.
> Tell me the same old story
> When you have cause to fear
> That this world's empty glory
> Is costing me too dear.
> Yes, and when that world's glory
> Is dawning on my soul,
> Tell me the old, old story —
> Christ Jesus makes thee whole.

THE GOSPEL IS THE POWER OF GOD

Paul wrote his letter to the Roman church when Rome ruled the world. It was the capitol and center of the first century world, and its legions were everywhere. Yet in this very godless city, there was a Christian church. No one knows who started the church at Rome, but it certainly wasn't Peter as the Roman Catholics claim. There's no historical evidence at all of Peter leading this church, let alone of him spending twenty-five years as its bishop.

The Lord's people in Rome were a mixture of all sorts; slaves and wealthy. It must have been a deeply spiritual church for Paul to be able to write to them such a mighty theological epistle. The letter reveals the unbelievable sinfulness of man, the indescribable glory and holiness of God, and particularly the power of the gospel to save sinners. To a sophisticated, sin-riddled city like Rome, this would not be very impressive. They were impressed with military might and conquering force, and probably dismissed the gospel as weak and irrelevant. Realizing this, at the beginning of his letter Paul makes it very clear that he is not ashamed of the gospel. In going to Rome, he knew that he would face intense opposition. To a measure he faced this everywhere, but Rome was a cesspool of every foul thing imaginable. The terrible sinfulness of man pictured in chapter one had reached its pinnacle in Rome. In such a place it would have been very tempting to have watered down the gospel to make it more acceptable, or come to the people with a message they wished to hear. The gospel, in spite of the fact that it's good news, is the most hated and opposed message the world has ever heard. That's because it doesn't merely say, "God loves you and wants you to spend eternity with Him in heaven." That's only half the gospel, and to preach only that is to be a false prophet. It's to preach, "Peace, peace," when there's no peace.

The gospel always starts by talking of mankind in sin. Only then does it say, "God loves you and can deal with your sin and save you." People don't like hearing the message of sin. No one likes being told they are wrong on any point, but to be told, as the gospel does, that our whole life is totally wrong is unacceptable. Indeed, the gospel even goes further than that. It denounces the long cherished belief of arrogant man that he has a free will and is master of his own destiny. The gospel says this is wrong. We're guilty and condemned and, left to ourselves, can do nothing about it.

This is too much for man and he reacts against the gospel with ridicule and persecution, among other things.

But the most dangerous reaction of all is to change the gospel, to water it down and remove its offensive parts. Thus, to end up with the unbiblical message that sin doesn't matter because we are all God's children and are all going to heaven.

Paul was aware of this and quite deliberately he writes, "I am not ashamed of the gospel." Here is a man speaking from white hot conviction born of experience. On the road to Damascus, with one blow, he had all of the props of good works, religious observance and privileged race knocked from beneath him. He met Jesus, the glorified Christ, and from then on had only one message: *salvation by grace alone through Christ alone*. He will hear of nothing else, and he speaks and lives nothing else. Far from being ashamed of the gospel, he glories in it.

In Romans 1:16-18, the apostle gives three reasons why he's not ashamed: because the gospel is the power of God for salvation, because in it a righteousness from God is revealed; and because it deals with the wrath of God.

POWER

The gospel is the power of God to save, and this is the sinner's only hope. Imagine sinners hearing the gospel. Initially, they will almost certainly react against it. They will not like its message and find it offensive. What it has to say is exactly what they need, but they cannot see this and reject it. How are such people ever going to be saved? The answer is that the gospel doesn't take "no" for an answer. It perseveres and will eventually triumph because it's the power of God to save. The gospel isn't merely a proposition put before man, nor is it merely a suggestion with only the power of persuasion. Rather, it has the dynamic power of Almighty God to accomplish what it sets out to do, namely, to save the sinner.

Such is the reality of the bondage to sin that man is in, and such is the power of sin in every human being's life, that nothing short of the greater power of God could make any one of us a Christian. The gospel is the most powerful thing the world has ever experienced—and is at its most lethal when being preached. It's powerful when read on the page of Scripture, but God has so ordained that its full power is seen in the preaching of its message. The devil is well aware of this, and therefore uses great energy to restrict preaching. In the early church, God's enemies in Acts 4 didn't forbid the Christians to meet together, worship or pray, but they did forbid them to preach Christ.

When Paul says he is not ashamed of the gospel, he really means that he's proud of it, delights in it, and glories in it. What is unique and extraordinary about this message that so excites the apostle? Paul gives the answer in Romans 1:16-18. First, it's the power of God for salvation. Secondly, it alone provides men's and women's greatest need: a righteousness to make them acceptable to God. Thirdly, it alone deals with their greatest problem: God's wrath upon them because of sin. The gospel does these things not by presenting men and women with moral and philosophical concepts for them to aim at, but by exploding into their lives with the transforming life-giving power of God.

WHAT IS THE GOSPEL?

It's the good news about Christ. It's the message of what God has done in and through the Lord Jesus Christ to deal with man's sin and to make the guilty sinner acceptable to a holy God.

True, the gospel has many sub-messages, but, in essence, it's not about Christ healing our bodily diseases. He may do that, but that's not the gospel. If it were, there would be no offense in it. Neither is the gospel about Jesus solving our marriage, emotional or financial problems. The gospel is about Christ dealing with our sin. Sin involves the cross, and the cross is always an offense to sinful man because it accuses us, judges us, condemns us—and leaves us in no doubt that we are guilty before God. This is the offense of the cross, but the glory of the cross is that it's our only hope of salvation.

We can see all this in Paul's own experience. Before he became a Christian he was a deeply religious, moral, sincere and honest man who hated Christ and despised the cross. How could such a man ever be saved, and why should such a man need saving in the first place? Paul tells us why he needed saving. All the morality and religion he had confidence in became for him nothing but a load of rubbish (Phil. 3:4-11). Sin makes us self-centered, causing us—if we are "religious"—to always look at what *we* are doing, what *we* are thinking and what *we* believe. It always fails to ask, what does *God* think of me? What does *God* require of me?

This power of spiritual blindness has to be broken before a man can be saved, and the only thing that can break it is the power of the gospel. The gospel points us away from ourselves and forward to Christ, His cross and resurrection. It makes us ask, why did Jesus die like this? Why did God allow it? Why such humiliation and agony? And why the resurrection? Religion can come up with plenty of pathetic answers to these questions, but the gospel alone provides the answer that satisfies the deep longings of the soul of man. Jesus died in our place. He died to remove the guilt and punishment of our sin, and he did so because God planned it. As we sinners hear these things, the power of God begins to work. Love and grace melt our hearts. A longing for pardon and salvation is created. We believe, and conviction is deepened until there's only one thing to do: come in repentance and faith to Jesus.

THE GOSPEL MEETS
MAN'S GREATEST NEED

The second reason that Paul gives for not being ashamed of the gospel is that it alone meets man's greatest need. Of course, it may be debatable as to what this need is. People define it in different ways depending on their position and circumstances. If you were to ask someone in a war-torn country, "What is your greatest need?," he would say, "End the war, finish all the blood shed and killing." If you were to ask someone from a famine-plagued country in Africa, he would answer, "Our greatest need is for food, our children are starving, our people are dying. Give us food!" One of the millions in our own country who are out of work would answer differently. He or she would say, "I want the dignity of being able to go out to work and earn a wage." A different answer would come to the same question from someone in a hospital bed suffering from a terminal illness. His answer would be, "My greatest need is for good health."

You can understand all these answers, but they are all dictated by *circumstances*. There's a need, however, that over-rides all circumstances. It supersedes the problems of all peoples wherever they are or whatever situation is confronting them. The greatest need, whatever our circumstances may be, of all people everywhere is to be acceptable to God. All men and women are made by God, for God, and all must answer to God. If there was no more war in the world, no more hunger, full employment, and everyone's health was perfect, people would still need the Lord Jesus Christ, because they are all sinners under the Judgement and wrath of God.

MAN'S PROBLEM

The problem for us all is that God is holy and we are not. There's no sin, no fault, no blemish in God, and He will not tolerate our sin. Man, as he is, doesn't satisfy God's demands, he cannot meet God's standards, and he is unacceptable to God. Many people find this difficult to believe and think that they make a reasonable effort at pleasing God. But the fact is that all man's righteousness is like a pile of filthy rags in the sight of God.

Imagine a man cleaning the engine of his car—it's filthy, and after he has finished mopping the oil off the metal work, the rag he is using is in a terrible state. His wife then calls him in because their little daughter has been sick in the house. He comes in with his dirty, grimy rag and mops up the mess. You can imagine the state of the rag by now. Then he goes into the den and puts the rag on the coffee table. If he acted like that, his wife would be very angry with this and tell him to get that filthy rag out of the house! That's what God says when we bring our righteousness to him. If a housewife quite justifiably feels revolted at the sight of that filthy rag in her house, so, too, does God when we bring our righteousness to him as if it's something to be proud of and worthy of salvation. God's opinion of us all is stated in Romans 3:10 where we are told, "there's none righteous, no, not one." That being the fact, man's greatest need is to be capable of meeting God's standard and being acceptable to him.

GOD'S ANSWER

The Bible tells us that the very righteousness we need is revealed in the gospel of the Lord Jesus Christ. Note that word *revealed*. The gospel is not man's idea of what religion ought to be, neither is it the result of centuries of man's search for God. The gospel is an announcement from heaven. It's God shouting from heaven, "Here is the answer to your sin and depravity and lack of righteousness!"

Righteousness in Romans 1:17 doesn't describe something about God like His holiness and love. It really means a righteousness that God gives us. It comes from God to us. That is why the gospel is "good news." It doesn't tell us what we must achieve: it tells us what has been achieved for us—and what we must now receive as a gift from God.

The gospel is designed by God: it's worked out by God, its purpose is to satisfy the demands of God, and its achievement is our salvation. But, and here is the key point, our salvation couldn't be achieved if God's demands were not satisfied.

GOD'S DEMANDS

So what are God's demands? God demands from us a righteousness that's as good as His own. We might think that this is unreasonable, but it's not. God made man sinless, in His own image, and God wants us to be as He made us. That's not unreasonable. But it's impossible— our sin makes it impossible.

Where then does that leave us? It leaves us with no ability or capacity to save ourselves. It leaves us needing some- one to save us. But whoever this Savior is to be, He will have to provide for us a righteousness as good as God's. The problem is that there's no righteousness as good as God's. So the only possible way we can be saved, the only possible way we can be acceptable to God, is if we have God's own righteousness. The demand would appear to be impossible to meet, but the gospel makes the impos- sible possible. God provides for us the very righteousness He demands from us.

We get this righteousness through the Lord Jesus Christ.

Jesus is God become man, the Son of God, coequal with the Father in glory, majesty, holiness and righteousness; and He came into this world to satisfy the reasonable, but impossible, demands of God on our behalf. For thirty-three years he rendered a perfect obedience to the law of God. He was the spotless, sinless, holy, Lamb of God. And because he had no sin, God was able to lay on Jesus the sin of us all. He took our guilt and punishment when he died in our place on the Cross.

God justly demanded that our sin should be punished, and it was punished at Calvary: the punishment fell on our sin-bearer and not us. In this way, Jesus satisfies all the demands of God on behalf of His people—the debt has been paid and God will never require it to be paid again.

BY FAITH

This righteousness comes from God to us by faith in the Lord Jesus. Now faith doesn't in itself save us, it's the righteousness of Christ that saves us. But that righteousness comes to us by faith. Faith is the vehicle by which we receive it.

In Philippians 3, Paul reminds us what he was like before he became a Christian (v.4-9). Paul's main problem was that, though he was very religious and desperate to be acceptable to God, he was trusting in what he calls "my own righteousness" which was the result of keeping the law. His problem was exactly the same as that of most of us: he kept bringing that pile of filthy rags into God's presence and saying to God, "Look how wonderful these are." He didn't see them as filthy rags. He called them "my own righteousness," but they were filthy rags in God's sight.

Faith is the exact opposite of that. Faith rests on the righteousness of Christ. It has seen its own righteousness as a load of rubbish. Faith sees nothing except Jesus, but what a wonderful sight Jesus is. Jesus, bearing our sin and guilt. Jesus, facing the wrath of God instead of us. Faith delights in Jesus, faith loves Jesus, faith trusts Jesus. Faith sees no hope of achieving salvation, but every hope of receiving it as a gift.

In the seventeenth century, a Scottish preacher named David Dickson said that he had taken all his bad deeds and put them in a heap, and taken all his good deeds and put them in another heap, and fled from them both to Jesus. That's what faith is.

THE GOSPEL ANSWERS
MAN'S GREATEST PROBLEM

Romans, chapter one, verses 18-32, is one of the most solemn and frightening parts of Scripture. It shows us the depths of sin in the human heart and God's holy re-action against it. If sin is a reality, then so too, is divine wrath, and the only answer to God's wrath is God's love in the gospel. Paul is not ashamed of the gospel because it answers man's greatest problem: the anger and judge-ment of God upon his sin.

CATALOG OF SIN

The catalog of sin in the first chapter of Romans has a very modern ring about it. Sin starts with man suppress-ing the truth of God (v.18). If this is done, then there can be no absolute standards and everything becomes rela-tive. Nothing is right or wrong: everything is a matter of opinion, with every person doing his own thing. That's what happened in Paul's day, and it's rampant in society today. The Bible is ridiculed on TV and radio. What God says is dismissed as irrelevant—a very effective way to suppress truth is to ridicule it. The same is true in the education of our children where the curriculum is often biased against biblical truth. That's not only true in religious education, but also in the choice of books to be studied for English exams.

The list goes on: verse 21, God is rejected; verse 22, we are wise enough to put men on the moon, but foolish enough to create an Aids epidemic. Truth is called a lie, and lies are venerated as the truth (v.25). Verses 26-28 remind us that sexual perversion is now as acceptable as it was in Sodom—"Because of this, God gave them over to shameful lusts. Even their women exchanged natural relations for unnatural ones. In the same way the men also abandoned natural relations with women and were inflamed with lust for one another. Men committed indecent acts with other men, and received in themselves the due penalty for their perversion. Furthermore, since they didn't think it worthwhile to retain the knowledge of God, he gave them over to a depraved mind, to do what ought not to be done."

Our newspapers are full of the sin mentioned in verses 29-31. The catalog culminates in verse 32, and how apt this is of our day and age. We pay those who look after our bodies and minds very little and those who look after our souls even less. Yet those who debase and warp the morals of our young people through so-called art, culture and entertainment are paid vast sums. So we approve of them and encourage them.

PRESENT REALITY

The message of Romans chapter one is that man will not take God seriously, and therefore cannot take sin seriously. The result of this is that the wrath of God is being revealed. That's expressed in the present tense; it's not something reserved only for the future, but it's a present reality. God never excuses sin. If nothing else, the cross ought to convince us of this. On the cross, sin is not excused, but punished, and Jesus bore that punishment. There's a day coming called "The Day of Judgement" when the wrath of God will be poured out on all those who have not trusted in Jesus for forgiveness and salvation. Jesus said they will be cast into hell where they will—for all eternity—endure divine judgement. God's wrath is as eternal as His love.

All that's terribly true, but it's not what Paul is referring to in the first chapter of Romans. Here he is not talking about something future, but something present. God's wrath doesn't come now as it did in Noah's day, in a flood that destroyed all. Nor is it as in the time of Sodom and Gomorrah, when fire and brimstone fell on those cities. It comes now, says Paul, in a more terrible way. Three times in verses 24, 26 and 28 the apostle says, "God gave them over to their sin." He holds back his restraining grace and effectively says, "If you want sin, then have it; have your fill of it and see where it leads."

It's as if God says, "If you want to make sex the main thing in life, then do so, but see the results—tens of thousands of abortions each year to destroy its consequence, adultery to break down family life and Aids to kill people. If you want materialism, then have it, but there's a cost to pay—the rich get richer and the poor get poorer, with all the terrible social consequences of crime, unemployment and starvation in the third world."

People ask, "Why are things so terrible in society today?" Here is the answer: "God gave them over." A nation is made up of individuals, and how we live as individuals determines the fate of the society in which we live. Sex, drugs, crime and greed are destroying the world because we will not take sin seriously.

THE GOSPEL'S ANSWER

Many people think that education or social improvement are the answers to the needs of our age. But education is helpless to deal with the world's problems. In and of itself, it's a good thing, and it's better to have a good education than a bad one. But a good education cannot change what a man is. It can change him from being a dull sinner into a clever sinner, but it still leaves him as a sinner! More damage has been done in this world by clever sinners than by dull ones.

Better social conditions are also helpless to deal with

sin. We all need to work and strive for better and fairer social conditions for everyone, but living in a slum or a palace doesn't change a man's nature. Which is the most socially privileged family in Britain today? The answer has to be the Royal Family, but sadly we have seen in recent years that social privilege doesn't shield them from broken relationships.

The only answer to society's problem is the gospel, because it alone can deal with God's wrath against sin. In Romans, Paul deals with God's wrath right up until chapter three, verse 20, then he says, "BUT." From there, he begins to present to us the good news of what God has done.

Out of enormous love and concern for the very sinners He is angry with, God planned the amazing way of salvation. The whole plan revolves around, and depends upon, the Lord Jesus Christ. As far as God was concerned, and judged by His standards, there wasn't one single righteous person in the world. There was no human being He could call good. But God sent His sinless Son into such a world. So there was then in the world one righteous man. In other words, there was only one man God wasn't angry with because of sin. On the contrary, of Jesus, God said, "This is my beloved Son in whom I am well pleased." What did God do with the sinless Jesus whom He loves deeply? Did he make him ruler of the world and command sinners to obey Him? Did he exalt Him and have all men and women bow to Jesus? He could have done all these things legitimately, but He didn't.

Instead, He made Jesus a Man of Sorrows. He saw to it that His Son was despised and rejected by men, but that wasn't all. God himself turned his back upon Jesus and He didn't do it reluctantly. Isaiah 53:10 says, "It pleased the Lord to bruise him."

What possible explanation can there be for all this? The explanation is *the gospel*. On the sinless Jesus, God laid all the sins of the people He was going to save. Jesus became responsible to pay the debt incurred by our sin. On the cross, the Savior bore our sin and guilt, and the wrath and judgement of God that we deserve. Instead of falling upon us guilty sinners, the terrible divine wrath fell instead upon Jesus our sin-bearer, upon the only righteous and good man in the world.

Because Jesus was righteous and good, He was the only one who could bear our sin. That's why God sent Him into the world. If God was going to save sinners, there could be no alternative. On the cross, the judgement of God falls upon the beloved Son of God. Jesus dies forsaken by the Father; bearing our sin; in our place. He pays the debt we owed for all the laws of God we had broken—and all the sin we will ever be guilty of. Thus, the holy demands of God are fully met. Our sin is punished. Wrath is turned away from us; and the love, grace and mercy of God come to us instead. This is God's answer to human sin. This *is* the gospel.

It's the gospel that saved us, made us Christians, and, as these truths are continually turned over in our hearts and minds, refreshes us and keep us close to the Lord.

They help to keep us humble; it's impossible to keep the cross in view and, at the same time, feel we are something special.

> Upon the Cross of Jesus,
> Mine eye at times can see
> The very dying form of one
> Who suffered there for me;
> And from my stricken heart, with tears,
> Two wonders I confess:
> The wonders of His glorious love,
> And my own worthlessness.

They help us keep things in perspective. When, as Christians, we are going through a difficult time and circumstances seem to pile up against us, we may see an unbeliever who is enjoying more favorable circumstances and envy him. If we do, we are in fact envying a man who is going to hell!

The gospel reminds us that we have the most important issue sorted out. Circumstances will change, but the wonder of God's love remains a constant in our life, and nothing can separate us from that love.

EXTRAVAGANT LOVE

John wrote his New Testament letters when he was a very old man. In spiritual terms, he had seen everything. He had spent three years with Jesus, and he had heard first-hand the teaching of the Savior as well as having been a witness to the miracles. He was at Calvary. He was the first man to see the empty tomb on Resurrection Day. At Pentecost, he had received the outpouring of the Holy Spirit. He saw the amazing growth of the early church and also its persecution. All this had given John a great sense of God's love. His rich spiritual experiences had not made him smug nor had they fostered a sense of superiority over other believers. Quite the opposite, this old saint was always amazed and humbled when he recollected God's love for sinners.

At the end chapter two of his first epistle, John mentions being "born again." This is the very first act of grace in the sinner when the life of God comes into dead souls. The moment he mentions it, there's stirred in his spirit a sense of wonder at what God has done for him, and he launches into the tremendous statement, "How great is the love the Father has lavished on us, that we should be called children of God."

Lavished is an extravagant word. It speaks not of a carefully measured portion, but of abundant and overflowing mercies. God's love is truly amazing. God's wrath and anger is something we could understand; we are all sinners by nature and action; we have turned our backs upon God and gone our own way. Truly, we deserve judgement. We see the effects of sin everywhere. Are not all the wars and crime the result of human sin? And what about the violence and permissiveness of society? Is not the breakdown of family life and the misery and unhappiness of so many homes all the result of sin?

Man is a sinner and sin is lawlessness. We deserve God's judgement, but the gospel, while not ignoring sin and judgement, speaks of love lavished upon us by God.

LOVE'S OBJECTIVE

The great display of divine love in the gospel has but one objective—that we should be called children of God. Of course, to be called something is not necessarily the same as being it. So to make sure that we do not misunderstand what he is saying, John immediately and boldly declares that that's what we are. A Christian is a child of God. John is not speaking of something that may be true of us at some point in the future. This is what we are now, the moment we are born again and God lavishes His love upon us.

Every believer finds this both a humbling and thrilling statement. When we realize what we are by nature; when we think with sorrow of all our sin since we were saved, let alone the sin before, it's astounding that God should call us His children. But there are some people who do not find this astounding at all. They think that everyone is a child of God, and that God is the father of all human beings. Therefore, there's nothing surprising in this to them. The problem is that they chose to ignore the fact of their own sinful nature and the clear biblical teaching that sin is so horrendous that it separates us from God. God hates sin and will not tolerate it, and He has prepared a hell where sin and sinners will spend eternity. John is under no false illusions about man. He knows of man's condemnation by the law of God and of the reality of hell, but still he says that Christians are children of God. It's astounding!

"Children of God" refers back to the phrase "be born of Him." It means that there was a time when we were not children of God, but the new birth has led to a change of our standing before God. To be born again is the glory of the gospel because it goes to the heart of man's problem and deals with our sinful nature. Our problem is what we have: a sinful nature, and only the gospel can change that.

Imagine a man happily driving down the highway in his car. The car begins to shudder and sputter, loses power and eventually comes to a halt on the side of the road.

He gets out, looks at his car and deduces that something is wrong. He is no mechanic, but he knows that much. But what is wrong?

He immediately sees something wrong. The windshield is filthy, covered with the splattered remains of thousands of dead flies. This is something he can cope with, so he gets out his little yellow duster and soon has the windshield sparkling clean. He has fixed something that was wrong, so expectantly he tries the ignition key again, but the car will still not start.

Again, he inspects his vehicle and sees something else wrong. One of the tires is obviously under-inflated. He consults his handbook, checks the pressure in each tire and brings the pressure in all four up to the manufacturer's specification. He has fixed something else that was wrong and again tries the ignition key, but still the car won't start.

You may think that this is the silliest illustration you have ever heard. Nobody would be so stupid as that! Maybe, but that's exactly how most of us acted with regard to seeking to make our lives acceptable to God. We realized there was something wrong, something missing in our lives. So we tried to rectify it in all sorts of ways. We tried morality, culture, education, even religion. That's as foolish as our friend on the highway with his yellow duster and his foot pump. The problem with his car was that there was no power in the engine. It was lifeless. Likewise, what was wrong with us could not be made right by any self-effort. We were dead in sin and needed the life that comes from the Lord Jesus Christ alone.

LOVE AT WORK

God's love for us is not sentiment or pity. It's a love that deals exactly with the problem of our sin. John goes on in 1 John 3:5 to say of Jesus, "He appeared to take away our sins." This is crucial. We could never be children of God unless the guilt and penalty of sin is dealt with. The power of sin in our lives has to be broken. But sin's power is held firmly in the hand of the devil, which is why Jesus called sinners, "children of their father the devil" (John 8:42-44). The devil is not willingly going to relinquish this power, so the sinners predicament appears to be hopeless. But the gospel says, "The reason the Son of God appeared was to destroy the devil's work" (1 John 3:8).

All that the sinner needs—his sin to be taken away and the devil's power broken—has been accomplished by the Lord Jesus Christ. So lavished is not such an extravagant word after all. What Jesus has done for us is staggering. God's love brought Jesus from heaven to earth. At Bethlehem, He added human nature to His divine nature. God became man and identified Himself with sinners so that, as the sinless Lamb of God, He could take away our sins. God laid our sins on Jesus, and the Savior carried them to the cross to face their deserved punishment. Surely, John is right to talk of God's love being lavished upon us. In fact, "lavished" seems too small a word to describe what God did for us in Christ.

LOVE FOR THE UNGODLY

The Bible has a great deal to say about the love of God, but what exactly is it? What do we mean when we talk of "divine love"? Several years ago, I was preaching on the love of God at a baptismal service. One of those being baptized was a young woman who had persuaded her father to attend. He rarely, if ever, went to church, and when his daughter asked him what he thought of the sermon, he answered that it was the same old stuff about the love of God. His thinking was, "What was so special about God's love? Isn't that what He is supposed to do? It's the same old stuff." The poor man could not have been more wrong. The love of God is the most amazing thing there is. Every Christian knows something of the wonder of Paul's words in Galatians 2:20 that Jesus "loved me and gave himself for me." This love is not sentiment or an empty gesture. Rather, it does something very definite.

In Romans 5:6-8 Paul is concerned that we fully

understand what God's love means. After mentioning it in verse five, he proceeds in verses six to eight to define it in what must be one of the great New Testament statements on divine love. "You see, at just the right time, when we were still powerless, Christ died for the ungodly. Very rarely will anyone die for a righteous man, though for a good man someone might possibly dare to die. But God demonstrates his own love for us in this; While we were still sinners, Christ died for us." There can be no true understanding of God's love apart from the cross.

There's nothing vague or undetermined about God's love. The words "at just the right time" speak of the eternal nature of this love. It was planned in eternity and worked out to a divinely appointed timetable. Christ's death on the cross was totally planned by God. Divine love didn't originate at Bethlehem when Jesus was born, but it stretched back before the creation of the world. There had been many tokens of this love to men and women, but the cross was the most glorious demonstration possible, especially when we realize who the objects of God's love are. In Romans five, Paul describes the recipients of this amazing love as powerless, ungodly and sinners.

POWERLESS

This speaks of a total inability to do ourselves any spiritual good. If you are mowing the lawn with an electric mower and the motor burns out, the machine becomes powerless. You can adjust the blades, shout at it, or even give it a kick, but it will be of no use. It's powerless and totally unable to do what it was made to do. In terms of salvation, that's exactly what all men and women are like. We are completely devoid of any spiritual ability or strength to change our sinful nature.

The Bible says we are incapable of understanding spiritual truth—"The man without the Spirit doesn't accept the things that come from the Spirit of God, for they are foolishness to him and he cannot understand them, because they are spiritually discerned" (1 Corinthians 2:14). Neither are we capable of pleasing God or obeying his commands (Romans 8:7-8). It's because this is true that we find sin so easy to commit and holiness so difficult to follow. We know what God requires from us, but we are powerless to do it. This, of course, means that we are incapable of dealing with our own sin in a way that satisfies God. Therefore, salvation is way beyond our grasp.

"Powerless" means that, spiritually, we are helpless and hopeless. Yet this terrible truth only serves to magnify the wonder of God's love. It's to the extent that we realize how powerless we are that we appreciate the greatness of divine love. Because we are powerless, we have nothing in ourselves to trust and even less to boast in. It's at this point of hopelessness that the love of God meets us. The gospel is "good news" because nothing else could help us. The powerless man doesn't need lessons in morality to help him live better, or even new religious insights to help him think better, he needs saving. He needs someone to do for him what he cannot do for himself.

UNGODLY

To put it very simply, "ungodly" means that we are unlike God. Man was made in the image of God, but sin has shattered that image so that man is as unlike God as it's possible to be. Everything God is, we are not. Because of this we do not love God. In fact, Paul says in Romans 5:10 that we are *enemies* of God. This means that we are opposed to God and in conflict with him. Many people refuse to believe this, and point to their religion and their church attendance as evidence that it's not true. Most of us Christians did exactly that before we were saved, but now we see how shallow such protestations are. "Ungodly" means unlike God; no love for God; no desire for God—and opposed to God. It's very easy to test this to see whether or not it's true of us.

The vast majority of people say they believe in God, but it's clear from their lives that they rarely seek to obey his commands. This is true because in spite of what they say they believe, they are, in fact, ungodly. In the same way, many who go to church on Sundays refuse to take God seriously and dismiss His words as if they are of no consequence. How can a man be anything but ungodly if he denies and opposes the words of God? Such people have beliefs about God, and may be genuine in their attitude, but when they are confronted with the Holy God of the Bible they say, "If that's God, I don't want Him." By such a response they are opposing God and they do so because they are ungodly.

But the wonder of God's love is that He loves the ungodly. He loves those who oppose Him, hate Him and even deny He exists. If this wasn't true there could be no salvation for any of us.

SINNERS

What are sinners? They are powerless, ungodly men and women under the grip of sin. Sin is such a revulsion to God that he will not tolerate it, and it's so powerful that it renders all its victims powerless. If but one single act of sin should come from God, then instantly He would cease to be God. That's the awfulness of sin, and we are all sinners. The love of God is not the same old stuff, but the most amazing truth that God loves sinners, and this love he has proved conclusively. God's love is not a fanciful, sentimental concept, but a love that sent Jesus to deal with our sin by dying in our place.

THE WONDER OF GOD'S LOVE

A sinful, powerless, ungodly person comes to experience God's love by faith in the Lord Jesus Christ. Jesus is the one and only Son of God. He is the delight of the Heavenly Father. Jesus came into a sinful world yet never sinned. But this Jesus died for us. That's the depth of God's love. Paul, in illustrating divine love, points us not to the sinless life or teachings or miracles of Jesus, but to His death. He does this because this is how God demonstrates or proves His love for us.

The life of Jesus was perfect and holy and sinless. But it could not, on its own, save one single ungodly person. His teaching was amazing and it was no exaggeration to say that no one ever spoke with His clarity and authority, but all the parables and sermons on the Mount could not help a man to salvation who is powerless. Christ's miracles were startling and there was no doubt of their genuineness, even his enemies acknowledged that. But all these events could not save a sinner from the guilt and penalty of sin. In order to save us, Christ had to die for us.

This was necessary for several reasons, but one was the nature and power of sin. Its grip on human nature is total and its strength is death. It will take all to the grave, to death and to hell. If we are to be saved, that power has to be broken. On the cross, Jesus faced death for us. He faced it bearing our guilt and sin and He faced it in a weakness caused by Him being our substitute and sin-bearer. It was a weakness not known by Him before. In this state of weakness and humiliation, Jesus triumphed over death. He conquered it and abolished it for his people. The resurrection was the evidence of this great victory, and here we see again the wonder of God's love.

As we Christians look at the cross and take in all we

can of its meaning and accomplishment, it's breathtaking, thrilling and humbling. Such love should draw from us a love for the Savior that supercedes all other loves in our lives.

GOD'S PLAN

The apostle Peter, preaching on the day of Pentecost, explained the cross in terms of both the wickedness of man and the infinite love of God. He accused his hearers very clearly of putting the Son of God to death. Their sin was enormous and they were responsible for it, but overriding this was the plan of God: "This man was handed over to you by God's set purpose and foreknowledge; and you, with the help of wicked man, put him to death by nailing Him to the Cross" (Acts 2:23).

The death of Jesus, both with regard to its manner and its purpose, was set and determined by God Himself. It wasn't a last minute adjustment to a plan that was going wrong. It always was the plan as the many references and allusions to the cross in the Old Testament make very clear. To the Christian, this is a thrilling truth because it puts our salvation at the heart of God's will and purpose for this world. For the unbeliever, it reveals the folly of rejecting, not merely a doctrine, but the set plan of almighty God. The death of Jesus on the cross was so meticulously planned by God that, over a period of thousands of years, He alludes to it, and shows us it's going to happen—so that when it does at last take place, there should be no doubt as to its meaning. If all this is true, then we had better take it seriously!

CREATION

When God created the world, He did so meticulously and carefully, so much so that if things were only slightly different life on earth would be impossible. For example, our distance from the sun is exactly positioned to give the earth the correct temperature to sustain human life. If the average temperature of the earth was raised by only two or three degrees, the polar ice sheets would melt, and London would be under 20 feet of water. If our planet was 10% smaller or 10% larger, human life could not exist. In the same way, the 23.5 degree tilt of the earth axis is not some arbitrary thing, but necessary for life.

Such meticulous work was needed by God to sustain human life on earth and, in the same way, when God planned our salvation, He was equally painstaking. God's way is the only way and we cannot amend it without fatal consequences. Man is now discovering that his own foolishness and greed may be affecting the ozone layer— the barrier God put forty miles above the earth to protect us from the sun's killer rays. We are all aware of the danger to life if the ozone layer is harmed. We cannot play around with God's meticulous plans either in creation or salvation. We need the cross exactly as God planned it. There can be no variation, no amendments—and no changes. The cross is God's set purpose and we must accept it as such.

In the garden of Gethsemane the disciples, not understanding what was taking place, tried to prevent the arrest of Jesus by meeting force with force. Jesus stopped them with the warning, "But how then would the Scriptures be fulfilled that say it must happen this way?" (Matthew 26:54). Then He makes this statement concerning His coming death, "But this has all taken place that the writings of the prophets might be fulfilled." Over and over again the New Testament repeats the same truths, not merely in regard to the general idea of the Savior's death, but even to specific details such as the betrayal (compare Acts 1:16 with Zechariah 11:12-13).

WHY DID GOD DO IT?

There are two reasons why God planned our salvation as He did. The first is that He wanted to, and He wanted to because He loved us. The other reason is that God did it because He had to if we were to be saved. Without a Savior, all sinners will perish eternally. Both reasons are found in John 3:16, "For God so loved the world that he gave His one and only Son, that whoever believes in Him shall not perish but have eternal life." In other words, it's

God's love that makes the cross possible, and it's God's holiness that makes it necessary.

That God is love is a precious truth that is accepted by practically everyone, but the meaning we give to love is not always biblical. Modern man confuses love with sentimentality, and sees God's love as a sort of general benevolence which has no other purpose but our happiness. It then follows that God will not punish sin. Consequently, every notion of hell is dismissed as incompatible with the idea of a "God of love." Such thinking is seriously flawed because, although it's true that God is love, this is not the only thing that's true about God. He is also holy. The love of God as seen on the cross saves sinners, but what are they saved from? The Bible has only one answer to that: sinners are saved from perishing, from the consequence of their sin, from the wrath and judgement of God upon that sin. Why in John 3:16 are people perishing? Because God is holy and will not, and cannot, tolerate sin. In 1 John 4:9-10, we see both the love and holiness of God linked together: "This is how God showed His love among us; He sent His one and only Son into the world that we might live through Him. This is love; not that we loved God, but that he loved us and sent His Son as an atoning sacrifice for our sins." Why was it necessary for Jesus to be an atoning sacrifice or propitiation for our sins? Because God in His holiness had declared that the wages of sin was death. He will not wink at human sin or pretend it's nothing. It has to be dealt with in accordance to His own law. The atoning sacrifice, or pro-

pitiation, Jesus made on the cross satisfies the law of God
and thus satisfies his holiness. The word "propitiation"
means that, on the cross, bearing our sin and guilt, Jesus
faced the wrath of God instead of us, and fully paid on
our behalf the debt we owed to the broken law of God.
At Calvary, Christ made it possible for a holy God to be
propitious—or favorably inclined—towards us, even
though we sinners had broken His holy law. God dealt
with the problem of sin in the only way that could satisfy
His holy justice and enable Him to move in and break
the power of Satan in sinners' lives. The fact is that it's
the holiness of God that dictates the events on Calvary.
In his love, God decided to save sinners from the consequence of their sin, but it's God's holiness that dictates
exactly how this is done. A way of salvation had to be
found that in no way contradicts the character of God.
This means that sin must be punished and not just glossed
over.

THE ONLY WAY

Sin is essentially a rejection of the character and being
of God. It refuses God's way and is an insult to His holiness. It's a hatred of all God stands for. But no person
can live in this world apart from the ways of God. God
has made us in such a way as to need oxygen to live. If a
man puts his head in a plastic bag he will die because
there will be no oxygen for him to breath. There's plenty
of oxygen all around him but, by his action, he has

chosen to cut himself off from God's provision for life. He deliberately ignores God's way and the consequences are terrible.

In the same way, God has made a provision for our salvation. If a sinner is to be saved he needs love, grace and mercy, and these flow in abundance from the Lord Jesus Christ. The gospel is not a complicated message only understandable by theologians. It simply says, "You are a sinner and Jesus is God's one and only provision for your salvation; believe the gospel; repent of your sin; have faith only in Jesus and live." But many will not do this. They ignore the meticulously planned way of God and put their heads in a plastic bag called morality, good works or religion. God's way is the only way, but it's a sure way. God planned a perfect and foolproof way of salvation. It can save the young and the old, the clever and the dull, the rich and poor. No one is barred from it because of race or color. That way is through the Lord Jesus Christ, and it's called the gospel.

THE CROSS IN THE OLD TESTAMENT: ISAIAH 53

In Isaiah, there are four passages which are known as the Servant Songs—42:1-9; 49:1-13; 50:4-11 and 52:13-53:12. On several occasions, the New Testament quotes these to describe the ministry of Jesus. For instance, Acts 8 quotes Isaiah 53 and Matthew 12:17-21 quotes Isaiah 42. Isaiah was writing in about 700 BC, so how could he so accurately describe Jesus? There can only be one answer and it's that God was revealing these truths to the prophet. In chapter 53, Isaiah presents to us a remarkable description of our Savior's death. When the Ethiopian eunuch in Acts 8 was reading this portion of Scripture, he could not understand it, but his ignorance was dispelled when "Philip began with that very passage of Scripture and told him the good news about Jesus."

DESCRIPTION

Other parts of the Old Testament describe Jesus as "The Lily of the Valley," "The Rose of Sharon," "outstanding among ten thousand and altogether lovely." In fact, the exact opposite of Isaiah 53:2-3. "He had no beauty or majesty to attract us to Him, nothing in his appearance that we should desire Him. He was despised and rejected by men, a man of sorrows and familiar with suffering. Like one from whom men hide their faces He was despised, and we esteemed Him not." In Isaiah 53, we do not see Jesus as the Son of God in all His unique glory and majesty, but as man's sin-bearer dying on the cross in agony and shame. Isaiah doesn't paint a pretty picture, but it's the same Jesus that Solomon describes as "altogether lovely."

Isaiah had already described Jesus as "Emmanuel, God with us." What we then see in Isaiah 53 is what God came into this world to do. It's staggering and almost unbelievable, but certainly true. In verse 2, we see the humble beginning of His life. He grew up on the streets of Nazareth and no one paid any special attention to Him. He was like an insignificant root in dry ground; a piece of vegetation that seemed doomed to wither away, so He was scarcely noticed. King Saul, the first King of Israel, stood head and shoulders above other men, and therefore could not help but be noticed. King David had a very attractive physical appearance so that eyes would have been drawn to him. The Jesus of Isaiah 53 wasn't like that. In spite of this, there was a beauty and loveliness about His character, and one would have expected that this would attract some. But it wasn't so. We see in Isaiah 53 the complete and absolute humiliation of Jesus. This was Emmanuel, God become man.

WHAT HAPPENED TO HIM?

The whole picture is one of suffering. In His life, Jesus had been familiar with suffering, but in His death the suffering reached untold depths. The words the prophet uses to describe what Jesus had to endure are significant. He was stricken, smitten, afflicted, pierced, crushed, punished, wounded and oppressed. That's a frightening list. Worst of all, He did nothing to deserve it. He was God's righteous servant (v.11) who did no violence nor spoke any deceit (v.9). We might expect therefore that He would plead His innocence and demand justice, but no, "He didn't open his mouth; He was led like a lamb to the slaughter" (v.7).

WHY DID IT HAPPEN?

The answer to this is most extraordinary. It's so staggering that most people refuse to believe it. They say it's impossible and even immoral. Yet, Isaiah states the answer very clearly and gets an abundance of support from the rest of Scripture. It happened because it was God's will. Jesus was stricken by God (v.4) and "it was the Lord's will to crush Him and cause Him to suffer" (v.10). This brings us back to Acts 2:23 and the truth that the death of Jesus was in accord with God's set purpose. Christ's death and how He died was all part of God's plan. The plan is unfolded in Isaiah 53 and no less than ten times are we strongly told that Jesus died for us, instead of us.

Jesus was suffering not for any wrong He had done, but on behalf of the guilty. That is why there was no objection from Him. To say that Jesus died in the place of sinners is not enough. The Bible will not leave it there and insists upon using key words like "propitiation" and "blood" to describe what Jesus was doing on the cross. Isaiah 53 goes further. The atoning death of Jesus is shown to be one of humiliation. It wasn't a quiet dignified death, but the sinless Jesus was identified with the wicked (v.9) and transgressors (v.12). He is killed with criminals as if He is no better than them.

More than that, He is crushed (v.5) by the law and justice of God. In verse 5, the Authorized Version and the Revised Authorized Version use the word "bruise," but that's too weak a word to describe what was happening. A bruise is uncomfortable and leaves a mark, but crushing is agonizing and destroys. The Hebrew word is *daka* and used of people being trampled to death. This was the death of Jesus.

The reason for all this is summed up in verse 10—"the Lord makes his life a guilt offering." This is the language of the Old Testament sacrificial system and simply means that if a sinful man, under the wrath of God, would approach Him, he must first sacrifice a spotless innocent victim in his place. This did two things: it showed the man acknowledged his sin, and that he came trusting in God's way to make atonement for that sin.

The wonder of the gospel is that God now makes Himself an offering for our sin. He sacrifices not some animal, but His own Son; Jesus, the Lamb of God who takes away our sin. Once we see that, Isaiah 53 becomes clear. We are all guilty and under God's wrath, but because He loves us, God lays our sin and guilt upon Jesus and pours out His judgement upon our substitute, our sin-bearer. Jesus is the guilt-offering for our sin. It's the punishment of our Savior that brings us peace (v.5). The Bible says that there's no peace for the wicked, and this is so because of our sin. On the cross, Jesus deals with sin and this brings us peace.

The song begins in 52:13 on a note of praise and victory, and ends on the same note at the end of chapter 53. The cross is a great success story. Because of His death, Jesus now has an offspring. The offspring are the people whose sin He has borne. He sees this offspring (v.10) and He is satisfied that He has totally fulfilled all that God the Father wanted Him to do. He has justified many (v.11) and made the guilty acceptable to God. This was His purpose in coming into the world, and that task is now finished. When Philip explained this to the Ethiopian in Acts 8, the man's life was transformed and he went on his way rejoicing. This is the experience of all believers: Our joy and peace rests only upon what Christ has done for us.

THE CROSS IN THE OLD TESTAMENT: ZECHARIAH

Zechariah, along with Haggai and Malachi, was one of a trio of prophets the Lord sent to the remnant of His people who returned to Jerusalem after the Babylonian captivity. These were days of great spiritual weakness, and the people were in a low condition. Zechariah's ministry was therefore meant to encourage them. The prophet does this in the greatest possible way. He points them to the mercy and grace of God in the coming Messiah, the Christ. In fourteen fantastic Old Testament chapters, consisting of a series of visions, the New Testament gospel is set before us 400 years before Jesus was born. The great perplexing question for any sinner who feels the weight and burden of his sin is: "How could I ever be acceptable to a Holy God?" Zechariah 3 shows us that the answer is in being clothed with the perfect righteousness of Jesus. There can be no gospel without the doctrine of imputed righteousness, and in this vivid picture of the priest in filthy clothes, the prophet shows us God's answer to the yearning of our heart. Christ Himself is introduced in verse 8 as "my servant, the Branch," and the great gospel promise is that God "will remove the sin of this land in a single day" (v.9).

In 6:12-13, there's a lovely portrayal of Jesus as priest and king. David Baron says of these verses, "This is one of the most remarkable and precious Messianic prophecies, and there's no plainer prophetic utterance in the whole Old Testament as to the Person of the promised Redeemer, the offices he was to fill, and the mission He was to accomplish." The Palm Sunday entry of Jesus into Jerusalem is shown in 9:9 and quoted by both Matthew and John. The betrayal of Jesus by Judas is foreseen in amazing detail in chapter 11:12-13. All this reminds us that there wasn't anything vague about God's plan of salvation. Nothing takes God by surprise because he planned it. In chapter 13, two truths stand out, both essential for our salvation and both reassuring for guilty sinners. The fountain and the sword speak of the grace and justice of God working for us.

THE FOUNTAIN

The Lord has opened a fountain to deal with sin and impurity. This fountain of grace and mercy makes life-giving water available to guilty sinners. The idea of God being a fountain of grace to His people didn't originate with Zechariah. In Psalm 36:9, David says of God, "For with you is the fountain of life; in your light we see light." The Lord complains through Jeremiah of the people forsaking this fountain—"My people have committed two sins; They have forsaken me, the spring of living water, and dug their own cisterns, broken cisterns that cannot hold water"(Jeremiah 2:13).

The fountain is a vivid illustration of the fullness and never ceasing mercy and love of God. Zechariah 13:2-6 reveals the emptiness of formal, man-centered religion. In contrast to this pathetic charade, the fountain really does cleanse from sin and impurity. Here's something that works. At the end of the twentieth century people are despairing at the blatant and arrogant march of evil. Crime of all sorts abounds and the largest group of criminals are teenagers. People are asking the politicians to do something, but they are as useless as the false prophets of verses 2-6. The only answer is God's fountain of grace and love. To open this fountain cost God an infinite price because the fountain is the blood of His Son. The proof of this is to be seen in verse 7, "Awake, O sword, against my shepherd, against the man who is close to me!," declares the Lord Almighty. "Strike the shepherd, and the sheep will be scattered, and I will turn my hand against the little ones." There's no doubt that this text refers to the cross because Jesus quoted it in Matthew 26:31-32 a few hours before Calvary and applied it to His death.

THE SWORD

In verse 7, it's the Lord Himself who is speaking, and He is not talking to any person, but to the sword. In Scripture, the "sword" is a symbol of judicial power. The sword which is the instrument of violent death is also the symbol of justice, so in Romans 13:4 a ruler is called the one who bears the sword. The Lord is calling upon the sword of judicial power not to defend, but to strike God's own shepherd. This shepherd is "the man who is close to me," or as another translation puts it, "the one who is my companion" or "kinsman." C. F. Keil writes, "God would not apply this epithet to any godly or ungodly man whom He might have appointed shepherd over a nation. The idea of nearest one (or fellow) involves not only similarity in vocation, but continuity of physical or spiritual descent, according to which he whom God calls His neighbour cannot be a mere man, but can only be One who participates in the divine nature, or is essentially divine." Specifically, the shepherd is Jesus, God's one and only Son.

Almighty God calls the sword of judgement to smite His Son. The teaching here is clear—it means that the death of Jesus was a judicial act. He endured the just and proper penalty of God's law upon sin which is death. It was the sheep which had sinned, not the shepherd, and it was therefore the sheep who deserved the sword's blow. But the shepherd interposed Himself and offered His own heart to the sword. He bears their sin upon the cross and dies in their place. It's God who instigates this; God planned the cross. God laid on Jesus our sin. God made Jesus to be sin for us. God delivered Jesus up for our sin. God opened the fountain. Sin is such a vile and terrible thing that nothing less than the death of a holy and sinless substitute could free us from its grip. The Son of God was the only one qualified to die for sinners. The dam of divine wrath broke upon Jesus our sin-bearer at Calvary, and the fountain of grace was opened.

The last words of chapter 13 are thrilling for any believer. It's because of both the fountain and the sword that we are able to call upon the name of the Lord with confidence. God answers that call with the most reassuring of all words—"They are my people". And it's only on the basis of God owning us as his that we are able to say, "The Lord is our God".

GETHSEMANE:
PROPHECY BECOMES REALITY

Immediately to the east of Jerusalem lies the deep Kidron Valley, which separates the city from the Mount of Olives. Late on the Thursday night, after leaving the upper room and the remarkable events of the Last Supper, Jesus, with the eleven apostles, crossed the valley to the garden of Gethsemane. There in that quiet place more remarkable events took place that set the scene for the first Good Friday. What took place there, apart from Calvary itself, is surely the most awful and solemn happening recorded in Scripture. Here we are shown the most private and intimate feelings of Jesus as He prepared Himself to face the cross in a few hours time.

The Bible is full of prophecies about the death of Christ. God pulls no punches as he describes in terrible detail the events that were to take place in such passages as Psalm 22 and Isaiah 53. But Gethsemane is not prophecy, it's the fulfillment of God's plan. Jesus is not now in heaven inspiring David and Isaiah to write their prophetic words, He is in Gethsemane, and the Cross is only a short distance away on the other side of the city. Spurgeon said of Gethsemane, "Here we come to the Holy of Holies of our Lord's life on earth. This is a mystery like that which Moses saw when the bush burned with fire, and wasn't consumed. No man can rightly expound such a passage as this; it's a subject for prayerful, heart-broken meditation, more than for human language. May the Holy Spirit graciously reveal to us all that we can be permitted to see of the King beneath the olive trees in the garden of Gethsemane!"

The hour had come and the awful reality of what is required to purchase our salvation is made evident. Jesus had always known what was required, but now he begins to feel it. Gethsemane is very much about feelings, about deep emotions. Jesus said, "My soul is overwhelmed with sorrow to the point of death" (Matthew 26:38). Luke tells us that the intensity of the feelings was such that Jesus sweat drops of blood (Luke 22:44). Mark says that Jesus began to be deeply distressed and troubled (Mark 14:34). Hugh Martin writes that "these expressions are far from conveying the great force and emphasis of the original." Martin goes on to say, "Here we have the grief of him who is the ever-blessed God; the sorrow and weakness and fear and trembling of Him who is the Lord God Ommipotent; the tears, prostrate agonies and cries of one who is now seated on the right hand of the majesty in the heavens, angels and principalities and powers being made subject to Him!"

It was no easy thing Christ was going to do for His people. Dying was one thing, but dying a substitutionary atoning death is something quite unique—and only the Lord Jesus Christ ever had to experience that. The cost of salvation is as immense as the love of God is deep, and both of these are seen in Gethsemane.

WHY WAS JESUS IN GETHSEMANE?

Jesus went there to pray (Matthew 26:36). It was a quiet place and Jesus often went there with his disciples (John 18:1-2). Prayer to Jesus was like breathing—it was the most natural of activities. But this time there were vital reasons to pray. He was about to face such experiences as no one had ever known. The events of Calvary were monumental. They were such that even Jesus was in deep distress at thinking of the prospect of them and his only relief was prayer. Prayer is not an escape from problems, but a facing up to them in the presence of God with an acceptance of His will.

Before going to Gethsemane, Jesus spoke about the experiences that He was to face. He said in John 14:30, "for the prince of this world is coming." Calvary was to be the great battle ground of eternity. Satan and all his hosts were ready to do their utmost to foil Jesus in his mission of salvation. What a scene must have been in the mind of Jesus when he uttered these words. He saw the prince of darkness assembling his legions of hate and evil, and all were set in array to hurl themselves at the Son of God.

Frightening though that prospect was, there was something even more terrible that was to happen at Calvary. Jesus knew that after Gethsemane He would not be able to call upon heaven to help Him because God was about to smite Him. God would lay on Jesus the sin of His people, and all of heaven's wrath against sin would fall upon Him as our sin-bearer. Both heaven and hell would be pounding Jesus. All this was about to break upon Him, so He needed to pray. God didn't let him down and sent an angel to strengthen Him (Luke 22:43). Remember that Jesus was the incarnate God. He said that all power in heaven and earth was given to Him. That this was no idle boast was seen in his ability to raise the dead, heal the sick, calm the storm and walk on water. Jesus is the omnipotent God. How then can an angel strengthen the omnipotent one?

TWO NATURES

Jesus is the God-Man. Probably the greatest mystery of all is that in Jesus there existed two natures. They were both real and equal, one didn't detract from the other. Before Bethlehem, Jesus was in heaven with God, and He was God. His divine nature knew nothing of the frailty and temptation of human nature. At Bethlehem, God became man. This was emphasized by Isaiah's prophecy that they would call the new-born babe Emmanuel, which means "God with us." The divine nature took to itself human nature. This wasn't a blending of two natures; it wasn't a mixture of the human and divine. Jesus is not part God and part man. He is both fully God and fully man, as much God in the manger as when he created the world.

Both the deity of Christ and his humanity are essential for our salvation, but as Berkhof said, "Men have sometimes forgotten the human Christ in their reverence for the divine. It's very important to maintain the reality and integrity of the humanity of Jesus by admitting his human development and human limitations. The splendor of his deity should not be stressed to the extent of obscuring his real humanity."

It was because Jesus was man that he could die and could feel the anguish of all that was involved in his atoning death. He needed strengthening and in Gethsemane God the Father sent an angel to do that. Jesus needed it because he was feeling as never before the terrible cost of salvation. The writer to the Hebrews tells us that, "During the days of Jesus' life on earth, He offered up prayers and petitions with loud cries and tears to the one who could save him from death." He felt things in Gethsemane He had never felt in heaven. He began to feel the weight of human sin that was to be laid upon him and the weight of divine justice that would also come. So he prayed with loud cries and tears. One of the old writers, Traill, wrote "He filled the silent night with his crying, and watered the cold earth with his tears, more precious than the dew of Hermon, or any moisture, next unto his own blood, that ever fell on God's earth since the creation."

This is why he needed the angel's strengthening, and the angels' ministry to Jesus probably consisted of reassuring him that this was God's will, and that there was no other way. Did the angel also remind Christ that the cross wasn't the end, but that resurrection would follow? In his weakness, Jesus needed to know from heaven that, though for a few hours He would be forsaken by God, but not for one minute would he cease to be loved by the Father.

But the man Jesus needed something else also. He needed the support and comfort of His apostles. When He went to the garden to pray, He didn't go alone—He took the apostles with Him not as a matter of courtesy, but because He needed them. This was particularly true of Peter, James and John. He said to them "stay here and keep watch with me." But they failed him. We can see his obvious disappointment when he found them asleep, "Could you men not keep watch with me for one hour?"

These three, who had experienced the glories of the transfiguration, could not share in the agonies of Gethsemene. They slept while Jesus agonized. The Savior was being driven more and more into isolation. A year before most of his disciples had left him (John 6). Soon the apostles would do the same thing, and the most terrible of all desertions would come when the Father would forsake Him. In Gethsemane, the tidal wave of God's wrath because of our sin is beginning to build up.

LIKE A FLINT

In the third of Isaiah's four Servant Songs (50:4-11), the prophet sees the Messiah setting His face like a flint to go to the suffering that the Lord had set for Him. He is determined to be totally obedient to the will of His Father. In Gethsemane, despite the intensity of His sorrow, Jesus wasn't seeking to avoid the cross. In fact, going to this particular garden was making the cross inevitable. We read in John 18:2-3, "Now Judas, who betrayed him, knew the place, because Jesus had often met there with his disciples. So Judas came to the grove, guiding a detachment of soldiers and some officials from the chief priests and Pharisees." Judas knew Gethsemane as a favorite spot of Jesus and was able to lead the soldiers there to arrest Him. D.A. Carson, commenting on this passage, says: "The time (at night) and location (away from the city itself, removed from crowds that could become mobs) provided the betrayer with an ideal venue in which to bring the arresting officers right up to Jesus. Having sanctified Himself for the sacrificial death immediately ahead, Jesus doesn't seek to escape his opponents by changing His habits. Instead, He goes to the place where Judas Iscariot could count on finding Him." Commenting further on the words in John 18:4, he goes on to say: " 'Jesus, knowing all that was going to happen to Him…' All four gospels present Jesus as knowing what would happen; e.g., in the Synoptics, the passion predictions, the agonizing prayer in Gethsemane and the calm insistence that He could call on legions of angels for help are otherwise meaningless. But the theme is especially strong in John; Jesus offers up His life in obedience to His Father, not as a pathetic martyr buffeted by the ill winds of a cruel fate." Jesus went willingly and obediently to the cross, but He went feeling deeply the cost involved in purchasing our salvation.

GETHSEMANE:
CHRIST'S DEEP SORROW

There's sorrow, and then there's sorrow. Some people are perpetually sorrowful and rarely smile. Their personality and nature tends automatically to pessimism. When you see such people in sorrow it's so usual to their normal state that you pay little attention to it. Others are of a much different temperament. They are always smiling and happy, so when they are sorrowful, it's so unusual that you have to ask, "Why?"

Neither of these two extremes was true of Jesus. He was the most perfectly balanced person there has ever been. When scripture describes him as the Man of Sorrows, it's not referring to his temperament, but to something very special that was to happen to Him. It's true that we are never told in scripture of Jesus smiling or laughing, but to draw major conclusions from that as to His temperament would be wrong. Jesus was the most normal man it was possible to be; He knew joy and sorrow. But the sorrow of Gethsemane had little to do with temperament.

The intensity of it was such that Luke says He sweat drops of blood. The night was cold enough for the soldiers to light a fire in the courtyard, yet Jesus sweat drops of blood. Mark says that the sorrow was such that Jesus was deeply distressed and troubled. This wasn't the sorrow Jesus experienced at Lazarus' death when He wept. Gethsemane was so different that even the Son of God was amazed at its intensity.

What caused such sorrow? J. C. Ryle said, "I believe the agony in the garden to be a knot that nothing can untie but the old doctrine of our sin being really imputed to Christ, and Christ being made sin and a curse for us." Ryle is correct and fully in accord with the teaching of Isaiah 53. Why was Jesus a man of sorrows? Because, says the next verse in that remarkable chapter, He carried *our* sorrows. He did that because the Lord had laid on Him the sin of us all. But in Gethsemane this had not yet happened. Jesus at that time wasn't bearing our sin; He wasn't yet facing the wrath of God instead of us; He had not yet become a curse for us. The sorrows of Gethsemane arose from the prospect and thought of the sorrows of Calvary.

THE CUP

Twice, Matthew 26:39,42, Jesus refers to what He is about to experience as "the cup," and it was the prospect of drinking from this cup that caused Jesus such deep sorrow. The sorrow wasn't caused by the thought of having to face death. Death wasn't the problem to Jesus that it's to us. He described it as having restored to Him the glory that he had with the Father from before creation. It was what was involved in the death that "the cup" refers to.

The idiom of drinking the cup in the Old Testament refers predominantly to God's punishment of human sin that the following verses make clear: "Awake, awake! Rise up, O Jerusalem, you who have drank from the hand of the Lord the cup of His wrath, you have drained to its dregs the goblet that makes men stagger." (Isaiah 51:17) "This is what the Lord, the God of Israel, said to me! Take from my hand this cup filled with the wine of my wrath and make all the nations to whom I send you drink. When they drink it, they will stagger and go mad because of the sword I will send among them." Jesus had always known that one day this cup of God's wrath would be put into His hand. But now in Gethsemane the concept is soon to become a reality and He feels something of the dread of drinking that cup.

MADE SIN

On the cross God lays on Jesus all the sin and guilt of His people. We can sometimes say this rather glibly without much thought or understanding as to how it felt for Jesus. How would you feel if you were made responsible for someone else's sin? And if that responsibility involved blame and resulted in punishment, how would you feel then? Yet the fact is that there's no sin that someone else may commit that all of us are not capable of committing. Sin is so much the dominant factor in our nature and behavior that we are actually capable of committing any wrong doing. But Jesus is the God-Man, sinless and perfect. Not only that, but He detested all sin—"your eyes are too pure to look on evil; you cannot tolerate wrong" (Habakkuk 1:13).

It was this Holy One who was made sin. When Jesus bore our sin and died, it wasn't theoretical, but very real. It had to be if the law of God was to be fully satisfied. A violated law would not accept a theoretical atonement. So when we say that Jesus was "made sin," what sort of sin did He bear? Paul in 1 Corinthians 6:9-11 reveals for us something of the burden that Jesus bore for His people—"Do you not know that the wicked will not inherit the kingdom of God? Do not be deceived; Neither the sexually immoral nor idolaters nor adulterers nor male prostitutes nor homosexual offenders nor thieves nor the greedy, nor drunkards nor slanderers nor swindlers will inherit the kingdom of God. And that's what some of you were. But you were washed, you were sanctified, you were justified in the name of the Lord Jesus Christ and by the Spirit of our God."

Hugh Martin writes, "True, the sins which were charged upon Him were not His own, but they were so laid upon Him and so became His, that He could not merely endure, but accept as righteous, the penalty which they entailed....And if the punishment of these sins was thus not in semblance, but in reality accepted by Jesus as justly visited upon Himself, must it not have been because the sins themselves had first been made His—verily, really His—to every effect save that alone of impairing His unspotted personal holiness and perfection? And if they were His to bring him wrath unto the uttermost in their penalty, must they not have been His to cause Him grief and sorrow inconceivable in their imputation? True, they were not personally His own; and so they were not His to bring self-accusation, self-contempt, despondency, remorse, despair. But they were His sufficiently to induce upon His holy soul a shame, humiliation, sorrow—yea, sore amazement—as He stood at His Father's tribunal, accountable for more (sin) than child of man can ever account for unto eternity."

SIN SEPARATES

The second implication of Jesus bearing our sin, is that if sin separates us from God, then it also separates our sin-bearer from God. Jesus knew this was going to happen. Therefore, when on the cross He cried out, "My God, my God, why have you forsaken me?," He wasn't merely quoting Psalm 22, but experiencing that awful separation. Jesus was to drink this cup of God's wrath to the very dregs. So fully did Jesus make Himself one with sinful man that He entered into the God-forsakeness that's the lot of all sinners: He died their death.

All this, and much more, was in the cup of God's wrath, and Jesus had to drink it all. There were no short cuts: this was the only way if men and women were to be saved from the guilt and consequence of their sin. The Old Testament Day of Atonement pictures for us what was taking place on the cross. In Leviticus 16, the Day of Atonement is described for us. In verses 7-10, we are told of two goats, one was killed and its blood was taken by the high priest into the Most Holy Place and sprinkled on the mercy seat, symbolizing the turning away of God's wrath from man's guilt. Mercy, instead of judgement, came to the sinner. The other goat, called the "scape-goat," was brought to the high priest, who laid his hands on the animal's head and confessed the sin of the people. Symbolically the sins were transferred to the scapegoat, and the goat, when sent into the desert, took away the sin of the people (v.20-22). All these things were symbolic. They were, says Hebrews 9:10, "external regulations applying until the time of the new order." That new order came with the Lord Jesus Christ. What was symbolic on the Day of Atonement becomes reality in Christ. The death of our Savior is the only sacrifice that God now recognizes. When Jesus died on the cross He did what both goats symbolized; He turned away the wrath of God from us and He took away our sin. It was the prospect of all this that caused our Savior such sorrow in Gethsemane. The cup was drained by the Lord Jesus.

Because of this, the Christian will never have to face this sorrow; we will never have to face the wrath and condemnation of God.

GETHSEMANE:
GOD'S WILL

There are two things uppermost in the mind of Jesus in Gethsemane. One is the awful prospect of being the sin-bearer for His people, and the other is the determination that God's will should be done. The deep sorrow that's overwhelming His soul is not the dominant force guiding the actions of our Savior. The sorrow is not warping what had always been His greatest concern, namely to do the will of His Father. He comes in prayer with His face to the ground in a spirit of reverence and awe. He is not demanding or pleading. The words, "if it's possible," are not to be interpreted as Jesus groping for a way out. He is merely making a request, but the request is couched in an acceptance that what really matters is the Father's will.

Neither is there any reluctance in the prayer. "We do not enter at all into the mind of Christ if we limit his language to a mere expression of his willingness to drink that cup which could not pass from him. We must understand the Savior as intensely desiring that the will of God should be done," says Hugh Martin. If Jesus is willing to accept God's will, why does he ask, "if it's possible, may this cup be taken from me"? Because the cost of God's will being done was immense to Jesus. The thought of what was involved prompts Jesus to ask if there's not another way. He knows the answer is no, and He is perfectly willing to accept this but it's putting him under enormous pressure. The sorrow was great in Gethsemane because of the great agonies He knew were awaiting him at Calvary.

WHAT WAS GOD'S WILL?

Jesus wasn't in disagreement with God's will, far from it. He is one with the Father in all things and, therefore, fully in accord with what God planned to do. On the cross, in the death of His Son, God was going to deal with human sin. There wasn't anything new about God dealing with sin. In Genesis 3, He dealt immediately with the sin of Adam and Eve. Their sin was exposed, judgement pronounced, and they were driven from God's presence. In Genesis 4, Cain was left in no doubt what God felt about him killing his brother, "my punishment is more than I can bear," he said. Then in Genesis 6:5-7, "The Lord saw how great man's wickedness on the earth had become, and that every inclination of the thoughts of his heart was only evil all the time. The Lord was grieved that He had made man on the earth, and his heart was filled with pain. So the Lord said, 'I will wipe mankind, whom I have created, from the face of the earth—men and animals, and creatures that move along the ground, and birds of the air—for I am grieved that I have made them.'" And so it was, right through the history of God's people. Israel in the wilderness knew God's dealing with their sin and so, too, did David after his adultery with Bathsheba. Sin pained and grieved the heart of God, but in one sense, those dealings in the Old Testament cost God nothing. He was punishing sinners, but he wasn't atoning for the sin, nor providing eternal salvation for the guilty ones.

It's true that God instigated a sacrificial system which symbolized atonement and salvation, but this system couldn't really deal with sin. It was, "an illustration for the present time, indicating that the gifts and sacrifices being offered were not able to clear the conscience of the worshipper. They were only a matter of food and drink and various ceremonial washings—external regulations applying until the time of the new order" (Hebrews 9:9-10). Additionally, we read: "The law is only a shadow of the good things that are coming—not the realities themselves. For this reason it can never, by the same sacrifices repeated endlessly year after year, make perfect those who draw near to worship. If it could, would they not have stopped being offered? For the worshippers would have been cleansed once for all, and would no longer have felt guilty for their sins. But those sacrifices are an annual reminder of sins, because it's impossible for the blood of bulls and goats to take away sins" (Hebrews 10:1-4).

These laws and pronouncements involved little or no direct cost to God Himself. God was deeply grieved by the sin of man, but the remedy cost man, not God. Demands were made for men to make atonement. God gave the instructions, but man had to provide the sacrifice. The dealing with sin at the cross was different. This cost God. Indeed, it touched the very being and person of God. He is not now merely making demands, He himself is providing the sacrifice and making the atonement. The sacrifice would be Jesus—and the atonement would be made through the shedding of His blood.

Now we face a seemingly impossible dilemma: At Calvary, God is not merely going to deal with sin by punishing it, He is going to provide full salvation for guilty sinners. But how can God do both these things? Sin must be punished; there can be no God-given salvation at the expense of justice—and the legal and just punishment for sin is the death of the sinner. So it would seem that justice leaves no room for salvation; they seem to be mutually exclusive. How can God be just, that is, deal with our sin as His law demands and as our sin deserves, and at the same time offer guilty sinners salvation? That's the dilemma.

SUBSTITUTION

The biblical answer to this seemingly impossible dilemma is the doctrine of the substitutionary death of Jesus.
Leon Morris says, "The richness of New Testament teaching on this subject centers on Christ. Was there a price
to be paid? He paid it. Was there a victory to be won? He
won it. Was there a penalty to be borne? He bore it. Was
there a judgement to be faced? He faced it. View man's
plight how you will, the witness of the New Testament is
that Christ has come where man ought to be and has
met in full all the demands that might be made on man."

The teaching on substitution in both Old and New Tes-
taments is vast and varied. In the Old Testament, we have
indications of this truth often in the historical narratives.
For instance, when Abraham was called upon to sacrifice his son Isaac in Genesis 22, God intervened and provided a ram to die instead of Isaac. It's seen more clearly
in the death of the Passover Lamb in Exodus 12, and
perhaps even more so in the details of the Day of Atonement in Leviticus 16. The great Messianic Song of Isaiah
53 tells us no less than ten times that Christ died for His
people—He was pierced for our transgressions, He was
crushed for our iniquities, the Lord has laid on Him the
iniquity of us all.

In the New Testament, the teaching is direct and clear:
"God made him who had no sin to be sin for us, so that
in him we might become the righteousness of God"

(2 Corinthians 5:21). Moreover, "He himself bore our sins on the tree, so that we might die to sin and live for righteousness; by His wounds you have been healed" (1 Peter 2:24), and: "For Christ died for sins once for all, the righteous for the unrighteous, to bring you to God" (1 Peter 3:18).

This was God's plan to deal with human sin. It was no theoretical arrangement, but was very real and very costly. It touched the heart of God because it cost Him the death of his Son. And the cost for Jesus was beyond imagination. God imputes or credits our sins to Him and He becomes responsible for them as our substitute. As our sin-bearer, He pays in full the punishment those sins deserve and faces the wrath and judgement of God. The awful reality of all this is heard on the cross when Jesus cries out, "My God, my God, why have you forsaken me?" He was experiencing what Psalm 22 could only imagine. We need to grasp the significance of this. He who hung on the cross had been for all eternity the object of God's love. And during the thirty-three years Jesus had been in this world He had enjoyed unbroken communion with God the Father. What then must it have meant for Him to be forsaken by God? The hiding of the Father's face was for Jesus the most bitter ingredient of the cup God had given Him to drink.

No wonder he cries, "if it's possible may this cup be taken from me." It would only have been possible if God were willing to give up His plan to save guilty sinners; if

God were prepared to scrap the plan made in eternity and prophesied in Scripture. Was this a dilemma for God? Would He forsake Jesus, His holy Son, or forsake us guilty sinners? As Christians, we can be eternally grateful that it was God who faced this dilemma and not anyone else. Anyone else would have understandably rejected us. But it was no dilemma for God. His love for us was so amazing and so wondrous that He forsook His Son in order to save us.

Some people have great trouble accepting this truth of substitution, even regarding the idea as immoral. Leon Morris answers them, "To put in bluntly and plainly, if Christ is not my substitute I still occupy the place of a condemned sinner. If my sins and my guilt or not transferred to Him, if He didn't take them upon Himself, then surely they remain with me. If he didn't deal with my sins, I must face their consequences If my penalty wasn't borne by Him, it still hangs over me. There's no other possibility. To say that substitution is immoral is to say that redemption is impossible."

It was God's will that sin should be punished, and the idea of an innocent substitute dying instead of guilty men and women was His. He doesn't expect us to provide an innocent substitute from among our friends—and anyway there are no innocents, for all have sinned. God demands a substitute and He, Himself, provides the substitute. God gives the only sinless Man to die for us.

CALVARY

The word "Calvary" is a very special one for Christians. This was the place Jesus died for them and purchased their redemption. The hymn writers delight in using the word, but surprisingly it's only found in the Bible once and that's in Luke 23:33 in the Authorized Version: "And when they were come to the place, which is called Calvary, there they crucified Him." In many modern translations the word is not found at all. They usually call the place "The Skull" or "Golgotha". All the versions are correct, the difference being that they take the name from different languages. The Aramaic word is *golgotha*. Calvary is the Latin translation of the Greek word *kranion*. Both the Latin and Greek words are translations of the Aramaic word which means skull. So probably the most accurate English translation would be "The Skull." But whatever name we use, it's the events that took place there that make the place special.

From Gethsemane to Calvary, Jesus says very little. It wasn't a time for talking, but for suffering. The sufferings of our Savior, physically, mentally, and spiritually were terrible but, strangely, the Old Testament tells us more of these than the New Testament. In the four Gospels, the writers continually focus our attention not just upon Jesus, but also on the people around the cross—Pilate, Herod, Caiaphas, the Pharisee and so on. We are shown their part in the crucifixion and their attitude towards Jesus, so that we may honestly examine ourselves before the cross of the Lord Jesus Christ.

THE CROWD

Luke tells us about the crowd and their leaders (23:35). The rulers sneered, scorned and made fun of Jesus. They made it abundantly clear what they thought and where they stood—they were against Jesus. The people, however, were more restrained; they stood watching. This was a public execution and it was a holiday time, so they came to watch. They were not bitterly and fanatically opposed to Jesus like their leaders; they just looked, curious, but rather indifferent.

Here were two seemingly different responses to the cross, but in God's sight there was no difference. Open opposition or just indifference to the crucified Jesus are both sinful and stem from hearts dominated by sin. The man who is an arrogant atheist and delights in mocking and abusing the name of Jesus, and the man who would not dream of doing such a thing, but is not committed to Jesus and just stands watching, (sometimes curious, sometimes indifferent, sometimes in church, sometimes not) are both the same in God's sight.

THE "IF" OF DOUBT

As you go through the events that surround Calvary you see that what links the various groups is the "if" of doubt. The rulers said, "if He is the Christ" (v.35); the soldiers, "if you are the king of the Jews" (v.37); the thief in verse 39 voices the same doubt, "aren't you the Christ." None of these believed that Jesus was God's Christ. They were spiritually blind: that's what makes a person either opposed or indifferent to Jesus. Both reactions stem from the same root of unbelief.

Jesus says in verse 34 that they don't know what they are doing, and Paul says in 1 Corinthians 2:8 that if they had known, they would not have crucified the Lord of glory. Does this ignorance excuse them or render them innocent? No, because they should have known. Plenty of evidence had been given them and they unintentionally acknowledged this when they said, "He saved others" (v.35). This ignorance reveals the deadly grip sin has on human nature. It blinds minds, deadens souls and enslaves the will and conscience. They didn't know—but they were still responsible.

Sin acts on us all the way that alcohol acts upon a drunken man—he doesn't know what he's doing. If he drives a car and kills someone he may truthfully be able to say, "I can't remember anything about it." But the law will still hold him responsible. And when a man dead in sin breaks the law of God, the Lord holds him fully responsible and demands that the penalty be paid. This is the terrible situation of all sinners, and it's a hopeless situation apart from the grace of God. It was because He loves us and sees our hopelessness that God sent His Son to deal with our sin and guilt.

GRACE AT WORK

There was one man at Calvary who realized who Jesus was; on that awful day he was able to rejoice with joy unspeakable. The penitent thief was an amazing miracle of grace. Even as the sky darkened and God forsook His Son, at that very moment, the angels of heaven were rejoicing over one sinner who repented.

In the story of the two thieves we can see God's sovereign grace in saving sinners. Both were physically near to Christ, both saw and heard everything, both were criminals who deserved judgement, both were dying men, both were sinners who needed forgiveness—yet one died in his sin and the other was saved. A fact like that ought to teach us humility. As Christians, we are no better than anyone else. The difference between the saved and the lost is the grace of God. It should also teach us a sense of urgency. It has been said of the two thieves that one was saved at the last moment of his life so that no one might despair, but only one so that no one might presume. Sinners need to be saved, and they need to be saved *now*. The work of grace in the redeemed thief follows the same path as it does in all the people of God. The steps of repentance vary little no matter what the sinner's background or circumstances. There are four:

1) **Fear of God (v.40).** Proverbs says that the fear of God is "the beginning of wisdom" and, we might add, it's also the beginning of salvation. It's a realization that we are answerable to a Holy God who will not tolerate sin; one who has said that no one who sins will enter His presence. It's the awareness that God means what He says and that He is not to be trifled with. Jesus said, "Do not be afraid of those who kill the body but cannot kill the soul. Rather, be afraid of the One who can destroy both soul and body in hell" (Matthew 10:28). The fear of God is the beginning of an awareness of the reality and presence of God, and of a true respect for Him. There's no salvation without this.

2) **Confession of sin (v.41).** Fear leads to confession. When we see God, we also see ourselves for what we are. We stop trying to justify ourselves and realize that our sin deserves hell. This conviction of sin will, in the grace of God, cause us to look for a Savior.

3) **Recognition of Jesus (v.41).** "This man has done nothing wrong," said the thief. In other words, Jesus is not like us. We are sinners, He is sinless. We are men, He is the Lord, the Son of God. He is our only hope and the only one who can save us. There are no "ifs" of doubt

here, just a quiet confidence in the ability of Jesus to deal with sin.

3) Prayer for mercy (v.42). This man was a criminal and therefore crucified by the Roman authorities. He was a sinner and therefore condemned by God. His situation was hopeless and he deserved nothing good. But he rested on divine grace and asked simply that Jesus would remember him. It's beautifully simple, to some it may seem too simple, but to be remembered by Jesus is enough. Christ's answer to this man epitomizes both His power and willingness to save sinners. The man was saved at the hour of the Savior's greatest weakness as He hung on the cross, forsaken by his Father. Surely, this is power. He was saved as a guilty sinner at the point of death with nothing in his past life to recommend him, and nothing in his present position except a prayer of repentance. In the morning he was a condemned criminal; in the afternoon he was a redeemed sinner, and by the evening he was a glorified saint in heaven.

THE MESSAGE OF THE CROSS

The gospel has always been a difficult message for people to believe and accept. The difficulty lies not in the gospel itself, but in men and women. Some may feel that such a statement is a cop-out made by Christians to explain the fact that most people reject the gospel. But this is not so. The gospel is unattractive and unappealing to people. They don't want it. This is not something new; Paul had the same trouble at Corinth in the first century. In the first chapter of 1 Corinthians, the apostle grapples with man's negative response to the gospel (v.18-25).

The message of the cross literally means the "word" of the cross. It's the Greek word *logos*. The same word is used in John 1:1, "In the beginning was the *Word*, and the *Word* was with God and the *Word* was God." It means all that the cross represents and stands for—it means the doctrine of the cross.

The biblical teaching about the cross started long before Jesus was born. The Old Testament messianic prophecies, for example, in the Psalms, Isaiah and Zechariah, are crucial if we are to fully understand the meaning of the cross. They are amazing in their accuracy and they point clearly to Jesus. When we come to the New Testament and the life of Jesus we find Him saying time and time again, that he was going to be put to death. He wasn't speaking in a mood of pessimistic fatalism, but because He knew that this was why He came into the world. Drawing on the Old Testament, Jesus likened Himself to the snake in the desert. "Just as Moses lifted up the snake in the desert, so the Son of Man must be lifted up, that every one who believes in Him may have eternal life" (John 3:14-15). By "lifted up," Jesus was describing His death on the cross (John 12:32-33).

Throughout the New Testament the message of the cross is clear. Peter said, "He himself bore our sins in His body on the tree" (1 Peter 2:24). John said, "the blood of Jesus, His Son, purifies us from every sin." In 1 Corinthians 1:23, Paul stresses, "we preach Christ crucified," and at the beginning of the next chapter (v.2) he makes the point that he resolved or determined to preach nothing else to the Corinthians but "Christ and Him crucified." Why did the apostle feel and act this way? It was because of the cross. If you are a Christian, the message of the cross is that Jesus took your sin, guilt and punishment. He faced the wrath and judgement of God instead of you and died in your place, and so God is now able to justly forgive you for all your sin.

No wonder the gospel is "good news." Could there ever

be better news? That instead of spending an eternity in hell, we can be accepted in heaven? By any reasonable standard, you would expect that people would be delighted with that. If there was a particular job about the house that needed to be done that I dreaded facing and kept putting off, I would be overjoyed if I got home and found that a neighbor had done the job for me. My gratitude would be enormous. I would rush to his home to thank my kind friend. That would be a normal reaction. So why don't people receive the message of the cross gladly?

FOOLISHNESS

Paul says, "the message of the cross is foolishness to those who are perishing" (1 Corinthians 1:18). This really is incredible. Here are people who are perishing. In Scripture, that means far more than death, it means that they are plunging into hell, forever to experience divine wrath. Yet these people, when they hear of God's guaranteed remedy to this, dismiss it as foolishness. Why do they act in this way? Paul answers this in the following verses. "Jews demand miraculous signs and Greeks look for wisdom, but we preach Christ crucified; a stumbling block to Jews and foolishness to Gentiles" (v.22-23).

The cross was God's only way of dealing in love and mercy with human sin. Jesus bore our sin, said Peter; God laid our sin upon Jesus, said Isaiah; God made Jesus to be sin for us, said Paul. All these verses speak of Jesus becoming the sinner's substitute and dying instead of us.

This is portrayed perfectly in the Old Testament scapegoat (Leviticus 16:8-11). The scapegoat on the Day of Atonement was the innocent victim taking away the sin of the guilty.

The Jews wanted proof. "Show us!….Prove it!," they were continually saying. Their pre-conceived notion of the Messiah as a great political and military leader made them reject Christ. A crucified Messiah was to them a contradiction in terms. Thus the cross was a stumbling block. The Greeks prided themselves in their superior wisdom and philosophical thought. They felt they were intellectually superior to everyone else. The cross was foolishness to them—it was outrageous and absurd. The response of these first century rejecters of the gospel is exactly the same as that of most folk today—preconceived ideas about themselves and God, and speculative thought about how God should and would act.

MODERN MAN

The message of the cross speaks of human sin and guilt, and of divine wrath and judgement. Today, people reject both sin and judgement, so they change the message of the cross. They sentimentalize it or shroud it in superstition so that the cross becomes nothing more than a lucky charm. Basically, men reject the cross as God's answer to human sin because they do not see sin as a problem. Therefore, there's no need for an answer. But the fact is that men and women are perishing and going to hell.

God warns us over and over again in the Bible of the terrible consequence of sin. The message of the cross comes to us with its invitation of salvation, but also with its warning if we reject the message—and yet still men reject it; they do not take their sin seriously.

During the Gulf War, Iraq launched Scud Missiles against Israel. These were terrible weapons that gave only one minute warning of approaching destruction and death. When that warning came, the Israelites fled to shelters for protection. Everyone ran for cover because they knew the danger was real. It would have been stupid to reject the warning and refuse the shelter.

The Christian is someone who has seen that he faces a far greater danger than that threatened by Scud missiles: he has seen his sin and takes it seriously. He has heeded God's warning and fled to Christ for shelter, forgiveness and salvation.

THE POWER OF GOD

The opposite of foolishness is wisdom, and therefore we would expect Paul in 1 Corinthians 1:18 to go on to say that for the Christian the message of the cross is wisdom. This he does later in the chapter, but not in verse 18. There he says that, to the saved, the gospel is the power of God. The gospel is not just some good advice telling us how we ought to behave. It's not even news about God's power—it **is** God's power.

In 1991, the Americans came up with an answer to the

Scud missile—it was the Patriot missile which could knock those terrible messengers of death out of the sky. This wasn't an infallible answer, for some Scuds got through. But God's answer to the terrible power of sin is infallible. In the cross, God did something that took tremendous power—He saved sinners. He destroyed the power of sin and Satan, and He now gives to His people the new life of the resurrected Christ. The cross demonstrates divine power as well as divine love.

When you consider Calvary and the power God had to exercise to save souls, it's amazing that people can think that good deeds, or a few Hail Marys, or baptism, or church attendance, or giving to charity can ever save their souls.

Christians are not saved just because they have all their questions and doubts answered. They didn't come to Christ in faith because their intellect was satisfied. While it's true that God never bypasses the sinner's mind in order to speak to the heart, the sinner is only saved because he or she is deeply convicted that they need saving, and that Jesus is the *only* Savior. The power of God in the gospel both convicts and saves. The Christian looks at the cross and cries with delight, "That's how God saved me!"

CHRIST LIFTED UP

When Jesus entered Jerusalem in triumph on Palm Sunday, the prophecy of Zechariah chapter nine was fulfilled. Calvary was only five days away. In John 12:27, Jesus said, "Now my heart is troubled." The prospect of the cross and all that it involved was proving daunting to the Savior, but He had no intention of avoiding it. He didn't ask His Father to save Him from the cross because this is the sole reason He came into the world. He came to die for *His* people, to give His life a ransom for us, and the cross was the God-ordained way this was to be done.

In verse 32, Jesus talks about being lifted up. John in the next verse adds an explanation of what the Savior meant. He was, says John, referring to the kind of death He was going to die. The kind of death Jesus was going to experience, or the way He was going to die, was most important. The way He died must clearly demonstrate who He was and what He was doing. Crucifixion was the only kind of death that could do both these things.

Stoning to death, the normal Jewish way of execution, would not.

Crucifixion showed who Jesus was because it fulfilled the Old Testament prophecies about the Messiah. Psalm 22, that great messianic passage, not only foresaw Jesus forsaken by His Father (v.1), the reaction of the crowd (v.7), and the behavior of the soldiers (v.18), but it also gives a remarkable description of the physical agonies of crucifixion—"I am poured out like water, and all my bones are out of joint. My heart has turned to wax; it has melted away within me. My strength is dried up like a potsherd, and my tongue sticks to the roof of my mouth; you lay me in the dust of death. Dogs have surrounded me; a band of evil men has encircled me, they have pierced my hands and my feet. I can count all my bones; people stare and gloat over me" (v.14-17). The Phoenicians were the first to devise crucifixion. They considered that all other means of execution were too quick. With crucifixion, men could die very slowly, it could take two or three days on a cross. The Jews never used crucifixion, but the Romans did, and developed it to an exact science with a set of rules to be followed.

Crucifixion showed what Jesus was doing. In Galatians 3:13, Paul said that when Jesus was hung on the tree (the cross) He, "redeemed us from the curse of the law by becoming a curse for us." Such a statement should cause every believer to gasp in wonder before the cross. The curse of the law is its penal judgement upon sin and, therefore, Jesus faced that instead of us. The Savior goes on in John 12 to mention three things that his death would accomplish:

1) The Judgement of the world (v.31). "Now," said Jesus, meaning not at the exact moment He was speaking, but in the whole proceedings of His death. The cross is the judgement of the world because in rejecting Jesus so viciously, the world was rejecting its only hope of salvation. To reject Jesus was to reject God.

At the same time He was uttering these words, Jesus told the parable of the Tenants: "Therefore, when the owner of the vineyard comes, what will he do to those tenants? He will bring those wretches to a wretched end, they replied, and he will rent the vineyard to other tenants, who will give him his share of the crop at harvest time." To reject the Son of God leaves men with nothing but the unending wrath and judgement of God. The same truth taught by Jesus in John 3 when he refers to the Old Testament incident of Moses and the snake in the desert. Sin brings judgement and "the Lord sent venomous snakes among them; they bit the people and many Israelites died" (Numbers 21:6). The only answer to this judgement of God was God's answer, which was to look to the bronze snake lifted up on a pole in the midst of them. Jesus said that this is a perfect example of what the cross means, but if men refuse to look to the cross as the provision of God's love and mercy for sinners, they will be left with their sin and its consequence.

2) The Prince of this world will be driven out (v.31). The "prince of this world" is a phrase that only Jesus used and He did so three times to refer to Satan (John 12:31; 14:30; 16:11). Satan is the "prince of this world" because he reigns in the hearts of men and women. Jesus acknowledges this by using the title. But men and women are God's creation, made in His image. Satan's reign is due to sin. Sin and death are his weapons and they seem to be invincible. D. A. Carson writes, "Although the cross might seem like Satan's triumph, it's in fact his defeat. In one sense Satan was defeated by the out breaking power of the kingdom of God even within the ministry of Jesus (Luke 10:18). But the fundamental smashing of his reign of tyranny takes place in the death/exaltation of Jesus. When Jesus was glorified, lifted up to heaven by means of the cross, enthroned, then too was Satan dethroned. What residual power the prince of this world enjoys is further curtailed by the Holy Spirit, the Counselor (16:11)."

3) I will draw all men to Myself (v.32). The lifting up of Jesus on the cross wasn't only the physical act of lifting His body on a piece of wood, but also involved the means of exalting and enthroning Him on His return to the Father in heaven. From His exalted position at the right hand of the Father, Jesus uses what was accomplished on the cross to draw men and women to Himself.

When Jesus said "all men," He didn't mean everyone without exception. He's not putting forward the teaching of universal salvation (atonement), because that would be to deny His many clear teachings that all will *not* be saved. "All men" means all *types* of people. Men and women from all nations, like the Greeks of verse 20, whose coming to Jesus prompted the whole discourse in John 12 about His death. The cross is the great proof of God's willingness to pardon sin. When Jesus died, it was to bring sinners to God not condemned by their sin, but pardoned by what Jesus did for them at Calvary. Drawing is accomplished by the preaching of the message of the cross. As sinners hear the message and are convicted by the Holy Spirit both of their sin and the hope of salvation, so Jesus draws them to Himself. He draws with great tenderness and love. He draws gently with the assurance that they will be received.

Jesus said, "No one can come to Me unless the Father who sent Me draws him" (John 6:44), but praise God he also said, "All that the Father gives Me will come to Me, and whoever comes to Me I will never drive away" (John 6:37).

THE TRIUMPH OF THE CROSS

On the cross, Jesus dealt with two things that opposed man and doomed him to spiritual bondage and eternal damnation. These two things are shown to us by Paul in Colossians chapter two. They are 1) *the law*—"having canceled the written code, with its regulations, that was against us and that stood opposed to us; He took it away, nailing it to the cross" (v.14), and 2) *the powers of darkness*—"And having disarmed the powers and authorities, He made a public spectacle of them triumphing over them by the cross (v.15)."

At the end of the twentieth century we hear a great deal about demons and exorcism. They are openly portrayed in books and films. Some folk are terrified by all this, others treat it as a means of entertainment. Many do not take it seriously and regard horoscopes, tarot cards and ouija boards as harmless fun. Some are puzzled by the phenomena, others reject it as medieval nonsense.

But to anyone who reads the Bible, this is not new or strange. Christ and His apostles often cast out devils. Mary Magdalene was said to have been possessed by seven devils. Moreover, the Bible teaches that all men and women, outside of Christ, are dominated and controlled by the devil (Ephesians 2:1-3).

Probably only a handful of people deliberately set out to worship Satan, but there are millions who ignore God and, therefore, whether they acknowledge it or not, are also living according to his dictates. There are also many who believe they are Christians, but they have never repented of their sin, never been born again, and it's of this type of person that Jesus said in John 8:44, "You belong to your father, the devil, and you want to carry out your father's desire." John's conclusion is that "the whole world is under the control of the evil one" (1 John 5:19).

All Christians were once in this condition. That's why Jesus came to save us. The law of God is against us, not because it's wrong, but because *we* are wrong. This gives Satan the power to enslave us and to accuse us before God. Satan wields the law of God to accuse and condemn us. Jesus came to change this by satisfying the law and paying the debt our sin had incurred, and by also breaking Satan's power.

SATAN

The reference in Colossians 2:15 to "powers and authorities" is to all unseen spiritual beings as in 1:16 and

2:10. But the verse refers specifically to Satan and his fallen angels; the powers of darkness as in Ephesians 6:12, "For our struggle is not against flesh and blood, but against the rulers, against the authorities, against the powers of this dark world and against the spiritual forces of evil in the heavenly realms."

The Bible has no doubt as to the actual personality of Satan. Many treat him as a joke, a comical figure dressed up in red tights with horns and a tail. It's noticeable in recent years how often ads on TV have utilized this comical figure to sell their goods. But Satan is no joke and neither is he an abstract power of evil.

There's never any question in Scripture but that he is a real person. It's important that we understand and believe this. Dr. Martyn Lloyd Jones wrote, "A belief in the devil and his powers is an absolute essential to a belief in the biblical teaching concerning sin and evil. You cannot really believe the biblical doctrine concerning sin unless you believe in the devil and in the principalities and powers associated with him. Further, a belief in the devil and his forces is absolutely essential to a true understanding of the biblical doctrine of salvation. 'Ah, but,' you say, 'that cannot be. Surely, all that's necessary is that I believe Christ died for my sins upon the cross.' So far you are right, but why did He have to come? What was He really doing on the cross? According to the apostle Paul, He was there, 'spoiling principalities and powers, making a show of them openly, and triumphing over them in it' (Colossians 2:15). Why did Christ have to come? One of

His own answers was this; 'The strong man armed keepeth his goods at peace, but when a stronger than he cometh upon him, he taketh from him all his armour in which he trusted, and divideth his spoils' (Luke 11:21-22). Do not think that you can understand the biblical doctrine of salvation and reject the devil. You cannot! You do not hold the true doctrine of salvation if you do not believe in the devil and his powers."

JESUS vs. SATAN

On the cross Jesus dealt with the law and bore the wrath of a sin hating God for us, but He also dealt with Satan and his all consuming grip on souls. At Calvary the most terrible battle of history took place. Jesus said on the night before the cross, "the prince of this world (the devil) is coming against me" (John 14:30). In this battle our souls were at stake as the satanic powers bombarded Jesus. In the darkness of mid-day and in the body and nature of man, Jesus battles for our eternal souls. The battle started at Bethlehem when Satan moved his puppet, King Herod, to try and kill the baby Jesus. It continued for the next thirty-three years as the temptation in the wilderness shows us, but it reaches its climax at Calvary.

Charles Spurgeon has an amazing passage in a sermon on Colossians 2:15. He said, "But the cross was the center of the battle; there, on the top of Calvary, must the dread fight of eternity be fought. Now must the Son of God arise, and gird His sword upon his thigh. Dread defeat or glorious conquest awaits the champion of the church. Which shall it be? We hold our breath with anxious suspense while the storm is raging. I hear the trumpet sound. The howlings and yells of hell rise in awful clamor. The pit's emptying out its legions. Terrible as lions, hungry as wolves, and black as night, the demons rush on in myriads. Satan's reserve-forces—those who had long been kept against this day of terrible battle, are roaring from their dens. See how countless are their armies, and how fierce their countenances. Brandishing his sword, the arch fiend leads the van, bidding his followers fight neither with small or great, save only with the King of Israel. Terrible are the leaders of the battle. Sin is there, with all its innumerable offspring, spitting forth the venom of asps, and infixing their poison fangs in the Savior's flesh. Death is there upon his pale horse, and his cruel dart rends its way through the body of Jesus even to his inward heart. One man—nay, tell it, least any should misunderstand me, one God stands in battle array against ten thousands of principalities and powers. On, on they come, and he receives them all."

TRIUMPH

The language of Colossians 2:15 is taken from a triumph of the Roman army. A victorious general would parade in triumph through Rome with the captured kings and generals chained to his chariot. In this way Paul depicts Christ's triumph over Satan: the evil one is defeated and chained to the chariot of our Savior. On the cross, Jesus disarmed Satan and took away his power.

Spurgeon in that remarkable sermon describes this disarming. "Satan came against Christ; he had in his hand a sharp sword called the law, dipped in the poison of sin, so that every wound which the law inflicted was deadly. Christ dashed this sword out of Satan's hand, and there stood the prince of darkness unarmed. His helmet was cleft in twain, and his head was crushed as with a rod of iron. Death rose against Christ. The Savior snatched his quiver from him, emptied out all his darts, cut them in two, gave Death back the feather end, but kept the poisoned barbs from him, that he might never destroy the ransomed. Sin came against Christ; but sin was utterly cut in pieces. It had been Satan's armor bearer, but its shield was cast away, and it laid dead upon the plain. Is it not a noble picture to behold all the enemies of Christ?—nay, my brethren, all your enemies, and mine, totally disarmed? Satan has nothing left him now where with he may attack us. He may attempt to injure us, but wound us he never can, for his sword and spear are utterly taken away."

As we saw in Zechariah 3, Satan is silenced by our new garment of righteousness. He can no longer accuse us because the law is satisfied in Jesus fully paying our debt. What a glorious triumph this is. On the cross, Jesus made a public spectacle of His victory. The whole world was witness to it, and still is every time a sinner is saved. The triumph of the cross was complete. Jesus had anticipated this on Palm Sunday when He said, "Now is the time for the judgement of this world; now the prince of this world will be driven out" (John 12:31).

The relationship between verses 14 and 15 of Colossians 2 is important. Man because of his sinful nature violates God's law. So the law instead of being a blessing to us becomes a curse. Therefore, Satan can quite properly use it to accuse and condemn us. We are guilty—"the power of sin is the law" (1 Corinthians 15:56). But on the cross, Jesus fulfills the righteousness of the law for us. He pays our debt and takes the cancel statement of debt, nailing it to the cross as proof of payment.

When we are saved, the triumph of the cross becomes our triumph. Satan can still tempt us, but he can no longer compel us. His influence is still strong in the world, but it's limited in the lives of God's people. He is chained like the lions in *The Pilgrim's Progress*. As Christians, we should live in the reality of the triumph of the cross. We are no longer slaves to sin so, therefore, we are not to let sin reign in our lives (Romans 6: 6, 12).

CRUCIFIED WITH CHRIST

In Galatians 2:20, Paul gives us a remarkable statement of what a Christian is. "I have been crucified with Christ and I no longer live, but Christ lives in me. The life I live in the body, I live by faith in the Son of God, who loved me and gave himself for me." He is not telling us what he did in order to become a Christian, but what was done for him and to him by Christ.

The Galatian epistle was written to counteract a heresy that had come into the church that taught the grace of God wasn't sufficient on its own to save sinners. Man's own efforts and good works, particularly circumcision, were also essential for salvation. This wrought havoc in the early church and divided the believers. Even Peter was caught up in it (Galatians 2:11-12). Paul denounces the heresy and clearly states that salvation is by grace alone through faith.

EXPERIENCES

Paul had many real and rich experiences of the Lord
Jesus Christ, but he didn't make the mistake of making
these experiences the foundation of his Christian beliefs.
Experiences come and go in any Christian's life. They
also vary from one believer to another, and are much too
flimsy and uncertain to be the foundation of anything.
The foundation of Paul's life and the explanation of all
that he was as a man and a Christian, were the doctrinal
truths about Christ and His atoning death.

Experiences should never be allowed to create doctrine,
but the value and authenticity of each experience is to be
judged by the unchanging truth of Scripture. An experience can be wrong, but biblical truth cannot be in error.
So Paul says, what happened to me is only to be explained
in terms of what the Bible teaches. Paul is the last person
you would expect to be writing the words of Galatians
2:20. He was born and bred a strict Jew and trained as a
Pharisee. His whole background was contrary to his
present position. He had hated Christianity and violently
opposed it, but on the road to Damascus he met Christ
and these words are his explanation of that meeting.

A NEW UNDERSTANDING

When he says "I have been crucified with Christ," obviously he is not speaking literally. The two thieves could
literally say, "I was crucified with Christ," but not Paul. If

Paul had been at Calvary he would have been one of those who mocked Jesus. He would have seen Jesus as a trouble maker who deserved to die, and the cross as just another execution. But now he knows he was wrong. Calvary wasn't primarily man doing something terrible to Jesus, but Jesus doing something wonderful for men. Paul's understanding of the cross was changed. He was brought up as a Jew to say, "Cursed is every one who hangs on a tree," but now with delight he identifies himself with the cross and declares that he is crucified with Christ.

He is saying that what Jesus did on the cross involved him personally. When Christ died, he died. He died to the wrath of God (Romans 5), and he died to the dominion of sin in his life (Romans 6). Paul gladly identifies himself with Christ's death because he realized that there's no salvation apart from this. This new understanding of the cross also gave him a new understanding of life. His life is now to be lived solely for the glory of God, and this means he is to be submissive to the authority of Christ. The *I, self, ego,* of the old Paul are dead. Christ now lives in him as his Lord and Master. "Christ lives in me" means far more than that he has changed his religion. It means that a living Christ is now controlling his life. Being a Christian is not trying to be morally better, it's a daily, living experience of the indwelling Christ. It's a real experience of a real Savior, so that we can say, "for me to live is Christ." Christ is everything to the believer, the lover of his soul, the bearer of his sin, and the Lord of his life. This is totally different from that of nominal church attendance. So how do we get this? Paul's answer is: "he loved me and gave himself for me."

THE WORK OF GRACE

"He loved me," is the heart of the gospel. It takes the gospel out of the general and makes it particular. It's a personal message from God that comes to us as individuals. That God loves me is not an inevitable deduction from the fact that God loves the world. Some make this deduction and therefore are not surprised that God loves us as individuals. This lack of surprise exposes a heart ignorant of the true nature of the gospel. It's an attitude that reduces the gospel to something ordinary and matter of fact, whereas in reality it's the most wondrous and amazing message.

He loved *me* brings before us the great element of grace in the gospel. When Paul said, "he loved me," he could never forget that he once tried to destroy the work of Christ. Yet God loved such a man. It was all of grace, not earned or deserved. The gospel always addresses itself to us as sinners who deserved nothing but judgement.

To say that God loves sinners is a tremendous thing, but it's not the whole gospel. The gospel is not just that Jesus loved me, but that Jesus loved me *and* gave Himself for me. The gospel erupts into its full majestic splendor at the cross. There's no true gospel message that doesn't include the atoning death of Jesus. God loving sinners doesn't in and of itself change anything. But when that love finds a way of dealing with man's sin and guilt, and the wrath of God upon that sin, and makes man acceptable to God, then everything is changed. Because of this, "I have been crucified with Christ and I no longer live, but Christ lives in me." Believing this and then coming in repentance and faith to God for forgiveness changes the sinner's whole standing before God. The truths of grace lead to the experience of salvation and new life in Christ. Faith and repentance bring pardon, pardon brings peace, peace brings joy, joy brings assurance—and all will eventually bring glory.

NO CONDEMNATION

No one likes to be condemned. Whether the condemnation is fair or not, it almost inevitably switchs on the defense mechanism of our pride to either flatly deny what we are accused of, or to attempt to justify our actions. This tendency in human nature is a major obstacle to someone believing the gospel. The word "gospel" means "good news," and the Christian gospel is the good news of what Christ has done for His people. But it will only be good news to those who take seriously the reality of their sin and the reality of God's holiness and judgement upon that sin.

If you read in the morning newspaper that a cure had been discovered for some fatal disease which had been devastating society, that would be good news. But unless you or a loved one suffered from that particular disease, you would forget the good news by lunchtime. You might not deny the news, but because it doesn't really effect your life it would soon be forgotten. So it's with the gospel. No condemnation is only good news if we realize we are condemned. Therefore, the first work of the Holy Spirit in sinners is to convict them of their sin and guilt, and the condemnation of God upon sin. This is why the Bible speaks so much about human sin and spells out consistently and clearly God's condemnation.

The Christian no longer defends his or her sin. Rather, Christians thank God that all sin is pardonable, but knows that no sin is excusable. There's no excuse for pride, envy, jealousy, gossip, thieving or adultery. There's no excuse for unbelief (Romans 1:20). The sinner is guilty and therefore condemned, but Jesus came to take the guilt of sinners and substitute in their life justification for condemnation.

Therefore, for the Christian, the gospel is the greatest news it's possible to hear. The consequences of being saved are staggering—acceptance with God, no condemnation now or ever, a guaranteed place in heaven. Believers often tend to minimize in their thinking the effects of salvation. That's why they get depressed and lose their joy and assurance. It's when we keep our eye on the cross and learn to rejoice in what God has done for us that our Christian life remains fresh and vibrant. In Romans 8, Paul having made the bold declaration, "there's now no condemnation for those who are in Christ Jesus," goes on to give the reason for this.

THE REASON

The reason is "because through Christ Jesus the law of the Spirit of life set me free from the law of sin and death." No condemnation is not because we have changed our life style and no longer sin so much. It's not because we are now better people and more religious. In fact, it's not because of anything we have done at all. It's because of what Christ has done in freeing us from the law that condemns.

Before we were saved we were under the law of sin and death. Law here means a regulating power or authority that governs our standing before the Holy God. The law of sin and death quite rightly condemns us and renders us unacceptable to God. The only remedy for this is the law of the Spirit of life, that is, the action or working of the Holy Spirit within us to bring us new spiritual life. The gospel takes us *out* of Adam and puts us *in* Christ. It's because we are in Christ that there's no condemnation. It's not our actions, but our standing before God that removes the condemnation. We are no longer condemned only because we have been justified. Justification is a sovereign work of God, and because of this it's a perfect and finished work. Because it's all of God there are no degrees to it. You are as justified the moment you are saved as you are ever going to be.

It's because of this that we can be confident that nothing can condemn us and thus rob us of our salvation.

This is the ground of assurance. Christian assurance doesn't depend upon sanctification, but justification. If it depended upon how spiritual or prayerful or obedient we were, it would be ever fluctuating—as unstable as we are. Because it depends upon what God has done for us in Christ it can remain as solid as a rock. Later on in Romans 8:34 Paul answers the question, "Who is he who condemns?" He does this by pointing us not to anything we have achieved, but to the atoning death, resurrection and intercession of the Lord Jesus Christ.

A WARNING

"No condemnation" doesn't mean that it is acceptable for a Christian to sin. We can never be condemned eternally because Christ has paid the debt we owed to the broken law of God, but we are still answerable to God for our actions and behavior. Eternal judgement will never be ours, but sin can rob us of much of the present joy of the Lord. Our sin can grieve and quench the Spirit, bringing dishonor upon the name of our God. We are not to "live according to the sinful nature, but according to the Spirit" (Romans 8:4). The grace of God that brought salvation to us "teaches us to say no to ungodliness and worldly passions, and to live self controlled, upright and godly lives in this present age" (Titus 2:11-12).

No condemnation is not an excuse to sin, but a reason to live for the glory of God; to please the One who loved us and gave Himself for us. It's both a staggering and humbling truth that ought to strip us of worldliness and plant in every believer's heart a determination to live a holy and godly life.

SAVED FOREVER

No Christian is sinless, and we probably have more trouble with sin after conversion than we did before. Sadly, we often give into temptation and feel very guilty. We may then begin to wonder if this sin will rob us of our salvation. But if justification has put us into a place where there's no condemnation, this must also mean that we cannot be separated from the love of God, which is exactly Paul's conclusion at the end of Romans 8.

There, he makes the confident declaration that nothing can separate the believer from the love of God. His confidence is based on the truths he has been expounding in Romans, particularly what he said in Romans 8:30: "And those He predestined, He also called; those He called, He also justified; those He justified, He also glorified." These are four mighty links in the chain of sovereign grace, one stretching back into eternity, two are experienced in this present life and the fourth, glorification, stretches forward into eternity. Each is as strong and unchallengable as the others, and each depends upon the mercy and grace of God. Thus the glorification, which is yet to be, is as sure as the other three that are already established facts in the life of every believer.

Jesus had already stated the same truth in John 10 when he declared that no one can snatch the Christian from his Father's hand. There the Savior reveals one of the greatest and most thrilling aspects of the gospel: once the sinner is saved, he or she is saved forever. It's impossible for Christians to lose that salvation and fall from grace, because they are eternally secure in the hand of Almighty God.

DIFFICULTIES

There are some Christians who have difficulty in believing this and some who totally reject it. They say that believers can fall from grace and lose their salvation. They explain the words of Jesus that no one can snatch them out of God's hand, by asserting that while this is true, it's possible for Christians to jump out of God's protecting hand. Such an explanation hardly deserves to be taken seriously, but it does reveal what is probably the real problem in rejecting the truth of eternal security, and that's the man-centeredness of some Christians' idea of salvation. They make the will of man, rather than the grace of

God, the corner stone of salvation. Preaching of this kind produces endless decisions for Christ, but because these decisions rest on mans acceptance of God rather than God's acceptance of man, it's inevitable that they don't last. The explanation then given is that they have fallen from grace rather than the biblical explanation that they were never saved in the first place.

The folk who believe that one can fall from grace appeal to certain passages, and these passages do deserve serious study—John 15:6, and Hebrews 6 and 10. But a serious study as opposed to a quick reading removes the problem. From the context you find that the passages are talking of people who never were believers. It's true that they had certain resemblance to Christians, but they are not true believers. In John 15:6 they didn't remain in Christ, that is, they didn't take their life and strength from Christ. The relationship to Him was superficial, merely a surface or nominal experience. The same is true in Hebrews 6. The key verse there is verse 9, "we are confident of better things in your case—things that accompany salvation." The warning this chapter gives is of people who come into close contact with Christ and the church, but never have a living experience of the Savior. Commenting on John 10:28, D. A. Carson writes, "To think otherwise would entail the conclusion that Jesus had failed in the explicit assignment given Him by the Father, to preserve all those given to Him. The ultimate security of Jesus' sheep rests with the good shepherd."

In John 10, Jesus gives reasons why the Christian cannot lose his salvation.

GIVEN BY GOD

The words used by Jesus in verse 29, "My Father, who has given them to me," spell out the true basis of salvation. (cf. John 6:37-39, 17:2,6,9). The subject all through the Bible is God's glory and our salvation. The glory of God in salvation is not that He foresaw who would respond to the gospel and be saved, and therefore chose them. The glory is that by His own sovereign will He chose for Himself a people before the foundation of the world. They are His by *His* choice *not* theirs—"They were yours: you gave them to me" (17:60).

This doesn't mean that the sinner has no choice or responsibility. We are told to seek the Lord and to receive Christ, but behind every action of man is the sovereign purpose of God. It's God who saves and who accepts us in Christ. From beginning to end salvation is the work of God, and the end of salvation is not the day we are saved, but that we may be presented faultless in His presence—in other words, glorification.

The God who has given us to Jesus "is greater than all" (10:29). For the Christian to lose his salvation, to be snatched out of God's hand, would mean that, first of all, Almighty God would have to be defeated and dethroned. But that's impossible because He is greater than all.

NEVER PERISH

What does the Good Shepherd give His sheep? Jesus says He gives them eternal life and adds that they shall never perish, neither by their own efforts or by all the powers of hell. The life which the common grace of God gives to men and women is life with a limit. It's limited by the influence of sin and death. But Christ on the cross conquered sin and death for His people, and the life we have in Him knows no limitation. It's eternal. This is what God gives us. Paul says in Romans 11:29 "God's gifts and his call are irrevocable."

The saved can never perish. They are secure by the continuing influences of the same Holy Spirit who first led them to believe. Their salvation is as secure as the infinite love, power, wisdom and faithfulness that the Almighty God can make it. That's some security! So Christians can rejoice that the One who saved them will keep them: they are safe in the loving hands of God.

QUOTES

ZECHARIAH

David Brown, *The Vision & Prophecies of Zechariah*, (Kregel 1975), p. 190

C.F.Keil, *The Twelve Minor Prophets*, Vol 2, (Erdmans 1965), p. 397

PROPHECY BECOMES REALITY

Spurgeon, *The Gospel of the Kingdom*, (Passmore & Alabaster, 1893), p. 237

Hugh Martin, *The Shadow of Calvary* (Banner of Truth, 1983), pp. 32-33

Louis Berkhof, *Systematic Theology* (Eerdmans, 1988), p. 318

D. A. Carson, *The Gospel According to John* (Eerdmans, 1991), pp. 576-577

IVP 1991

Trail quoted in David Brown's *The Four Gospels* (Banner of Truth, 1998), p. 332

CHRIST'S DEEP SORROW

J.C.Ryle, *Exository Thoughts on Matthew* (James Clarke, 1965), p. 362

Hugh Martin, *The Shadow of Calvary* (Banner of Truth, 1983), p. 40

GOD'S WILL

Hugh Martin, Ibid., p. 56

Leon Morris, *The Cross in the New Testament* (Paternoster, 1967), p. 405

Leon Morris, Ibid., p. 410

CHRIST LIFTED UP

D.A. Carson, Op. Cit., p. 443

THE TRIUMPH OF THE CROSS

Martin Lloyd-Jones, *Christian Warfare* (Banner of Truth, 1976), p. 50

Spurgeon, *New Park St Pulpit 1859* (Passmore & Alaabastor, 1894), pp. 386-388

SAVED FOREVER

D.A.Carson, p. 393

The Mission of Calvary Press

The ministry of Calvary Press is firmly committed to printing quality Christian literature relevant to the dire needs of the church and the world at the dawn of the 21st century. We unashamedly stand upon the foundation stones of the Reformation of the 16th century—Scripture alone, Faith alone, Grace alone, Christ alone, and God's Glory alone!

Our prayer for this ministry is found in two portions taken from the Psalms: "And let the beauty of the LORD our God be upon us, And establish the work of our hands for us; Yes, establish the work of our hands," and "Not unto us, O LORD, not unto us, but to Your name give glory" (Ps. 90:17; 115:1).

For a FREE catalog of all our titles,
please be sure to call us at:
1-800-789-8175
or visit our on-line store:
calvarypress.com